Missional. Monastic. Mainline.

Missional.
Monastic.
Mainline.

A Guide to Starting Missional Micro-Commmunities
in Historically Mainline Traditions

Elaine A. Heath
and Larry Duggins

CASCADE *Books* · Eugene, Oregon

MISSIONAL. MONASTIC. MAINLINE.
A Guide to Starting Missional Micro-Commmunities in Historically Mainline Traditions

Cascade Books
An Imprint of Wipf and Stock Publishers
199 W. 8th Ave., Suite 3
Eugene, OR 97401

www.wipfandstock.com

ISBN 13: 978-1-62032-624-4

Cataloguing-in-Publication Data

Heath, Elaine A., and Duggins, Larry

Missional. Monastic. Mainline. : a guide to starting missional micro-communities in historically mainline traditions / Elaine A. Heath and Larry Duggins.

viii + 138 p. ; 23 cm. Includes bibliographical references.

ISBN 13: 978-1-62032-624-4

1. Communities—Religious aspects—Christianity. 2. Mission of the church. 3. Missions—North America. I. Title.

BV601.8 H45 2014

Manufactured in the U.S.A.

For P.L.U.M.E.—the Presbyterians, Lutherans, United Methodists and Episcopalians in Alaska who are collaborating in missional community formation. May God take you on great adventures beyond your wildest dreams and through you, bring shalom to our world.

And for our students in the Academy for Missional Wisdom, those brave pioneers who are finding new ways to develop missional communities in their own neighborhoods. We give thanks for you. May your spirit be infectious in the one holy, catholic, apostolic church!

Contents

PART ONE

Why We Need Missional and New Monastic Communities In the Historically Mainline Church

1

How We Got Here

In this chapter we tell the story of how we met and how God called us into the ministry of creating new monastic and missional micro-communities and helping others in mainline traditions to do likewise.

Elaine's Story:

IN JUST THREE WEEKS Larry Duggins and I will take a group of divinity students to the U. K. for a Celtic monastic pilgrimage. We will pray, walk, sing, and listen our way to Lindesfarne, Glasgow, Iona, and Edinburgh in order to learn from and be inspired by gospel-bearing Celts. The class is part of a cross-cultural immersion program (Global Theological Education) at Perkins School of Theology, whereby students are exposed to understandings of life and faith that may be very different from their own. The hope for the GTE program[1] is that through cross-cultural immersions students' horizons will be expanded and their assumptions challenged about what is "normal," "traditional," and "right" in theology. This opening of the mind and heart begins with what

1. Global Theological Education, http://www.smu.edu/Perkins/Faculty Academics/Global.

students have learned in their home church, but goes beyond into what they have learned in seminary classrooms. Postcolonial theology, for example, takes on profound new meaning as they visit Palestinians and Jews in Israel, experience a Salvadoran Pentecostal house church, or meet young pastors in China. Advanced feminist theory means so much more as students encounter courageous South African women who challenge patriarchy in their own contexts.

The Celtic pilgrimage is a bit different from other immersion courses. In this encounter the cross-cultural experience has more to do with ecclesiology and missiology than anything else. We spend several days on the Isle of Iona, learning the stories of courageous monks of old who were martyred while evangelizing the Celts. There we also learn the history of the modern Iona community, with its focus on new monastic rhythms of prayer, hospitality, and justice. Our pilgrimage takes us through tough neighborhoods in Glasgow, where Reverend George MacLeod[2] first felt called to begin what is now the ecumenical Iona Community. There we cannot miss dozens of formerly busy cathedrals that stand in ruins, or that have been converted into pubs and museums. While sitting in a drum circle with members of the Wild Goose Worship Group,[3] or sharing the Eucharist in a Glasgow flat, students encounter the post-Christendom church in Europe. What they discover are small, very diverse communities bound together usually by a rule of life, a common interest in justice and prayer, and a deep unwillingness to engage in empire building in the name of church. Throughout the journey our student-pilgrims increasingly question the assumptions they have held about what constitutes the "normal" Christian life, the "healthy" church, and what it means to "make disciples." We have found that this pilgrimage haunts people afterward, creating a pervasive unrest with

2. For a good biography, see Ferguson and MacLeod, *George MacLeod: Founder of the Iona Community.*

3. Wild Goose Worship Resources is a ministry of the contemporary Iona Community, which is ecumenical, theologically progressive, and has both residential and dispersed members. See http://www.iona.org.uk/wgrg_home.php.

consumer forms of church, and it leaves a longing for simple community gathered around daily rhythms of prayer.

I met Larry Duggins in 2009, when he was one of the students who came on this very sort of pilgrimage to Iona. We were all at the airport, waiting excitedly for our departure. Some of the class had never been outside the United States. My colleague and friend, Michael Hawn, led the class with me. His expertise in global music and his friendship with several leaders in the Wild Goose worship group made this journey especially rich. While Michael chatted with some of the students I noticed one man whom I had yet to meet. I introduced myself and soon Larry and I were talking about his vocational goals.

With white hair and eyes that miss nothing, it was clear that Larry was not a first-career seminarian! When I asked what he hoped to do upon graduation, he said something about creating alternative spaces where young adults and students could experience worship and mission outside of traditional church. He wanted this new thing to be connected to the established church, but somehow in another space. Larry's description was on the vague side, but detailed enough to spark my immediate interest, because I was involved in this very form of community creation.

We had just completed our first year with New Day and the Epworth Project, two forms of intentional community that I had started with a few students and friends so that we could explore the potential for new monastic, missional, emerging ministry as United Methodists.

At the time New Day was one micro-church anchored in an established church. The lead team did not live together but we followed a common rule of life and shared all aspects of leading the community.[4] We met for worship and fellowship in a shabby but comfortable old house belonging to the United Methodist campus ministry. New Day that first year consisted of about fifteen

4. The development of our rule of life and a thorough testing of it formed the nucleus of Nate Hearne's doctor of ministry project. He later graduated with honors because of the importance of his project and the eloquence with which he wrote. I am deeply grateful to Dr. Hearne for his leadership role in the first year of New Day.

people, most of them students. We were primarily Anglo but with a few African American participants. We were still working toward figuring out what our mission would be, beyond offering an alternative form of church where students could learn about new monasticism and missional church. It would take another six months before we realized that our mission was among refugees and that we would need to move into the neighborhood where the refugees lived.

The Epworth Project was a residential community. Our first house, Alamo (named for the street it was on), consisted of three women students who lived together in Garland, Texas. The mixed income neighborhood was racially diverse but predominantly Latino. One of the women at Alamo House brought her golden retriever, Walker, into the house. It turned out that Walker was their best ally in forming friendly connections with neighbors, especially kids. Before long the Alamo House women were friends with many neighbors. The primary mission that emerged over those months was to serve elderly neighbors who needed assistance with various simple tasks, but who especially longed for conversation.

While we waited to board our plane to Scotland I shared with Larry about New Day and the Alamo House and what we were learning, and could see that he was intensely interested.

"We love what is unfolding," I told him. "But there is a problem. Last week the property owner who let us have the Alamo House this past year, rent free, said she suddenly needs her house back. The students have to move out of the house in six weeks, and we don't have another place for them to live. We are worried that we won't be able to continue the project, just when we were figuring out the best way to have intentional community of this kind. We really don't have money for a house. In fact, the way this house came to us was amazing. My friend and I had been praying for months for a house, when one day a neighbor I scarcely knew called and said she had a rental property that was vacant and she wondered if I might have a few students who would live there rent free for one to three years! She had no knowledge of what I am interested in, or the fact that we had been praying for a house. The neighbor said we would only have to pay the utilities and take care of the place. That's how the house came to us. Now we are losing it. So we are praying again about a house."

Larry stared meditatively into space.

Just then the announcement came over the loudspeaker that it was time to board the plane. As we flew out of Dallas and headed east I pondered Larry's keen interest and questions about our communities. I hadn't thought to ask him what line of work he had been in before coming to Perkins. We were too busy talking about our mutual passion for connecting young adults with a more meaningful expression of church. Our conversation was intensely energizing, so that I almost forgot we were in an airport and had somewhere to go!

Soon other matters occupied my attention, though, such as getting our group to the train on time, then the bus, and finally the ferry that would take us to our first destination. Forty-eight hours later we were on the beach in the "thin space" of Iona (a place where heaven and earth are uniquely close). I had just finished photographing the astonishingly blue water of the bay where dozens of monks were martyred, when Larry approached.

"My realtor has five houses ready for you to see," he said, holding out his iPhone. "Do you like any of these?"

I am sure that I looked as dumbfounded as I felt. I didn't know what to say. Was I hearing things? Who was this man?

Over the next two weeks as our class engaged in pilgrimage, as we prayed and sang, visited holy sites, journaled, shared meals and rides and met new friends, I gradually learned Larry's story. He had a background in the world of finance, where he had been a successful, effective businessman. Just a year earlier God had called him to leave the business world in order to go to Perkins School of Theology. He was now preparing for his new role as a spiritual leader. Most importantly, Larry was at heart a contemplative, deeply open to the Holy Spirit. He had been profoundly touched by some of Richard Rohr's teaching and had been a United Methodist for a long time. Larry was serious about finding a way for the Epworth Project to continue.

Thus our pilgrimage birthed a transition in Larry's understanding of his vocation, as God called him to come alongside in developing new forms of intentional community and new forms of theological education that could equip future generations of leaders for a post-Christendom world. What has happened since that day in the airport is astounding.

That first New Day community has multiplied into several communities around and near Dallas, all of them located in multicultural, missionally rich contexts. While New Day still offers learning experiences for many Perkins students every year, the communities are primarily comprised of lay people who are not students. The original New Day communities continue to evolve and adapt to their missional contexts, especially with refugees and with children living in poverty.

The Epworth Project has grown from Alamo House to seven communities across the Dallas/Fort Worth metroplex, each of them strategically placed for residents to live into a life grounded in contemplative practices and missional outreach. These residential communities have included a mix of students, persons working in non-profits for community development, refugees, campus ministers and clergy. Residents range in age from the early twenties to the mid-sixties and are racially, theologically, and economically diverse. We now have a generous scholarship program for persons who wish to live in an Epworth community while attending college or seminary, in order to learn how to live a missional, new monastic lifestyle.

Larry and I formed the Missional Wisdom Foundation—a 501(c)3—to provide administration of the Epworth communities, and to develop more initiatives through which to cultivate missional, new monastic leadership skills in participants. In 2011 we launched the Academy for Missional Wisdom, a two-year program for laity and clergy to learn how to start and lead these kinds of communities. The Academy is not for academic credit, and integrates distance learning with spiritual direction and local, on-the-ground training retreats. It is also portable, bringing the retreats and spiritual direction to the geographic area of each cohort. We have a wonderful team of instructors, all of who live the spiritual and missional practices we teach.

In 2013 we launched the next initiative, the Summer Immersion in New Monastic, Missional Life, which provided an opportunity for a dozen seminarians from as many schools to come together for a seven-week experience that combined intentional community, academic learning, missional service, and new monastic rhythms of life. Students lived, worshiped, learned, and served in intentional community with their instructors in Asheville, North Carolina.[5] This non-competitive opportunity was developed in collaboration with the Western North Carolina Conference of the United Methodist Church. It modeled the porous boundaries and collaborative learning among multiple institutions that we believe will be necessary for the future.

An Ironic Vocation

When I think about the trajectory of my life, or how I got here, in some ways it seems the most natural thing in the world that I should be doing this form of ministry today. But in other ways my vocation is deeply ironic. I grew up in poverty, in a virulently non-religious family fractured by alcohol and violence. Though my mother worked hard as a registered nurse, in those days nurses were paid very low wages, not enough to support a family of seven. My father was often unemployed or absent. We moved many times in search of something to lessen the wounds that drove the addictions in my father's life. Like all of my siblings, I left home when I was in my teens, a junior in high school. It was a move I made for my own safety. It is a miracle I ever graduated from high school.

---

5. Part of my inspiration for this program is the Oregon Extension, a wonderful semester long learning experience near Klamath Falls, Oregon, in which students from a consortium of thirteen Christian liberal arts colleges come to take three classes and live in intentional community. See http://oregonextension.org/.

As my family hopscotched back and forth across the Pacific Northwest, Montana, and Alaska, we encountered a few Christians along the way. How I wish I could find them today, to tell them what became of us! I wish that I could thank them. Some of them were public school teachers and some were neighbors. None of them were clergy. Each of these ordinary Christians with busy lives and other things to do, reached out to me with prayer, hospitality, and justice. They gave me an alternative community where I was welcome, a community of love where I belonged. It was through these few, short-lived encounters with people who acted a lot like Jesus, that I first experienced the kingdom of God. Those relationships started me on a trajectory that would eventually lead to deep healing, forgiveness, reconciliation within my family, and a vocation in theology. I came to Christ around the time I left home, and gradually over many years every member of my family, including my father, also became followers of Jesus. When my father died I presided at his funeral. I knew that his soul was at peace. My mother has become a woman of deep and profound prayer who is a great blessing to hundreds of friends. All of us thank God daily for the astonishing fact of reconciliation that binds us together in Christ.

Why am I here today, writing to you, and why am I committed to the formation of missional micro-communities? I am absolutely doing this work because I know how it is to be the "least of these," to grow up in the margins, to struggle to make ends meet and to long for something better but not know how to bring it about. I will always carry memories and consequences of experiencing multiple forms of violence. But more important than that, I know what it is to be transformed through Christian community that enfolds people like me with healing grace. I long for others to experience the love of God just as I have, and walk into the shalom that now marks my life.

Larry's Story:

You see, I was really planning on being a high school band director.

I loved marching band and I was a good enough trumpet player to compete on a statewide level in Louisiana. I had a wonderful high school band director in Douglas Bergeron, who challenged me and gave me lots of room to learn leadership and planning skills. During my senior year, I worked with Mr. Bergeron every morning, giving lessons to middle school kids and learning the logistics of choreography and planning. Everything was set—I would go to LSU in the fall to study under William F. Swor, whom I idolized, and I would learn to play and teach. But it did not quite work out that way.

During the spring of my senior year, Dr. Swor left LSU and was replaced by a man who, in the brilliance of my seventeen-year-old brain, I did not like. I had played in an Honor Band under Dr. Nick Rouse, who went on to become a dearly beloved director at LSU, and we had not hit it off well. I did not appreciate his style and I was too hardheaded to play under a director who rubbed me the wrong way. I went to LSU in the fall, but as an Arts and Sciences major.

I read philosophy and history, I studied Latin, I took "Physics for Poets." Mostly, I learned to be independent and to read and write critically. I took a degree in history, and moved directly into the Business School to pursue an MBA.

Because, you see, I was really planning on becoming a lawyer.

I was certain that the combination of a business degree and a law degree would position me to be a great lawyer in the business world. I thoroughly enjoyed my finance, economics and quantitative methods classes, and managed to live through accounting. I did well on the LSAT and applied to several schools, but I really had my heart set on the University of North Carolina. My letter finally came, and my young bride and I bundled up and moved to North Carolina, where I would become a lawyer. But it did not quite work out that way.

The letter I received told me that I was first on the waiting list for admission into the Law School. When I talked to the admissions folks, they told me that they had taken folks off the waiting list for years, so that I was a shoo-in to get a place. But for the first time in fifteen years, they did not take anyone off the waiting list. There we were, a young married couple living with my mom and dad, with no direction.

My wife Jay took a job as a legal secretary and I went to work as an audiovisual technician for a training firm, teaching presentation skills to executives at IBM. I stood behind the camera shooting video of executives sharpening their speaking skills, but it was not long before the consulting firm took me out from behind the camera and put me in front of it. The instructors taught me their methods, and before long I was coaching executives while running the camera. It was fun and it was a great skill to learn, but Jay and I were not happy and were having trouble finding friends, so we decided to move back to Baton Rouge.

Because, you see, I was really planning on becoming a banker.

I went back to LSU to take a second, more specialized masters degree in finance so that I would be well prepared to structure complex financial transactions with the captains of industry. Most of the business graduates from LSU at the time headed toward Dallas and Houston, which were the hubs of the Texas banking empires. so in January of 1984, Jay and I headed to Houston to work in the management training program of a big bank.

And we moved right into the face of the biggest banking crisis our country had seen since the Great Depression. First oil and gas prices plummeted, creating huge economic stress in Texas, followed almost immediately by stress on real estate prices caused by the savings and loan crisis. I was quickly moved from lending into workout, charged with salvaging as much value from broken loans as possible. One by one, the Texas banking giants fell, and I found myself working for the loan management subsidiary of an Ohio-based commercial bank, without ever having changed jobs!

My job was to figure out ways to help my employer maximize its return on the failed loans it had acquired when it bought a Texas banking firm from the FDIC, essentially working myself out of a job. I became aware of an interesting new financial structure that Wall Street was cooking up to allow commercial loans to act as collateral for bonds, and helped to devise a pilot securitization program for my bank. The folks in Ohio were interested, but very wary of the potential financial risks. The more I learned, the more that I saw a program with huge potential for asset management and investment management fees with relatively low risk. I could not convince my Ohio bosses that we should pursue this business, and I became increasingly frustrated.

Because, you see, I was really planning on becoming an entrepreneur.

In the spring of 1996, my friend Don Farmer and I left the bank to start our own investment analysis firm. We believed that we could capitalize on the opportunities that our bank had failed to seize, and we headed off to make it happen—and fairly quickly ran out of money. I found myself spending a lot of time explaining the idea to potential investors, who generally liked the idea but saw two struggling guys from Dallas as a risk in making it happen. Just as we were beginning to lose hope, one of the investors I had been courting forever finally told me that he could not figure everything out, but that he wanted me to talk with his partner Lee Cotton before we gave up. We talked on the phone, and then in person, and Lee got it.

And from that discussion sprang ARCap, which became one of the preeminent Special Servicers and high yield investors in the Commercial Mortgage Backed Securities industry. We had our share of growing pains—Don eventually went on to become a highly successful mortgage lender—but we were in the right place at the right time, able to help shape an industry and to find ourselves a highly profitable niche in a booming market. Lee and I consciously chose to run our firm according to our Christian principles, taking care of all of our people and making certain that our folks took a long-term view toward our client and investor relationships, treating everyone as fairly as we could. We gathered hundreds of millions of dollars of investment capital and ultimately controlled thousands of commercial loans totaling billions of dollars. And we were happy doing it.

After ten years, we kept a promise to our investors and sold the company to a New York based investment firm in order to realize the gains on their investments. It was a great day for us all—Lee and I made a lot of money, but more importantly so did our people. Because of our commitment to profit sharing, almost 20 percent of our people made more than one million dollars on the sale, and our receptionist bought her first house with her share.

Lee and I both stayed on with the acquiring firm, but after awhile, things were different. We had different constituencies to please and the market was becoming overheated. We were more and more concerned about the poor credit quality we were seeing in the marketplace, and we began to worry about storm clouds on the horizon. I was flying to New York two and three times weekly and I was exhausted.

Because, you see, I was going to become a pastor, which was the farthest thing from my mind.

One late night in March 2008, I was flying home from New York for the third time that week. I had gone through my normal routine by letting the flight attendant know that I would ask if I wanted anything, putting on my noise canceling headsets with meditation music, and doing my best to be anywhere mentally but in an airplane again. After an hour, the Holy Spirit spoke to me, not necessarily in an audible voice, but as clearly as if she were a person seated next to me. "Why are you doing this?" she asked. "How much more money do you need? How many more deals do you need to do? I have other things for you to do." I was rattled, but my direction changed. I retired from my position in June, and was in SMU's Perkins School of Theology by August.

I was raised as a Southern Baptist by good, God-fearing parents, but in college I had drifted away as many do. When Jay and I had our first child, Katie, we moved back into the church, but with a Sunday morning connection. When our second child, Chris, got big enough, we both started teaching Sunday School, but as he grew into middle school, my commitment to the church grew deeper. I taught Chris's Sunday school class for six years, which caused me to study the Bible more than I had in the past because I just could not make myself use the prefabricated lesson plans. I became an avid consumer of the Christian popular press, including the voices of the emerging church. Brian McLaren, Shane Claiborne, Rob Bell, and Jonathan Wilson-Hartgrove stretched my mind and helped me to imagine a church outside of the walls of the wonderful Methodist megachurch I attended.

I also found mission, accompanying the kids on the middle school and high school trips. I connected with Dusty Craig, a dynamic young youth pastor who preached wonderfully and sincerely in a way that was uniquely young and real, and in a way that reached the kids he was preaching to. I listened to the music of Micah Blalock, Dusty's very talented high school pal, as he led the kids into truly spiritual places as they sang and danced in praise of God. So I entered Perkins dreaming about empowering young people and connecting with them in a way that helped them to truly engage God.

Elaine has already mentioned the wonderful Global Theological Education program at Perkins, and I quickly resolved to participate in as many of those trips as my electives would allow. Over the course of my three years at Perkins as a Masters student, I traveled to Spain, Israel, Jordan, Egypt, Australia, Switzerland and France—but the most influential trip was to Scotland and England with Elaine and Michael. I tapped into the Celtic concept of Thin Places, places where the veil between earth and heaven is so thin that one can easily feel the presence of God. We visited Iona and Glasgow to see the Iona Community at work, and we stayed in northeast England with the Northumbria Community, where we fell into their pattern of daily prayer. My fellow travelers included wonderful spiritual people who still fill the role of *Anam Cara* for me today. I saw firsthand the amazing power of new monasticism to connect and empower people in the twenty-first century.

And I encountered the evangelical juggernaut who is Elaine Heath. She leads with enthusiasm, prays deeply, and listens when the Holy Spirit speaks. Those of us who are her students jokingly refer to ourselves as Heathens, but in a way that is a wonderful term. Elaine teaches us to follow the leading of the Holy Spirit and not to allow the impediments of hierarchy to hold us back, all while urging us to love "the tradition behind the tradition" (in my case, the tradition behind Methodism), and to bring health and support to our church as strongly as we can. The result causes us to often be a bit unorthodox, following in the footsteps of John Wesley, Phoebe Palmer, and other saints who follow the leadings of the Wild Goose of Iona.

With the benefit of hindsight, I can see the providence of God throughout my journey, giving me the tools and gifts I need, and bringing me to the places and people with whom I am to walk in God's service. That providence is what the Missional Wisdom Foundation is all about—listening to the urgings of the Holy Spirit to raise up a new generation of dedicated, committed, and faithful leaders, and running as fast as we can to keep up with her!

Conclusion:

As you can see, the two of us pretty much come from different planets! But God is all about bringing together a people who could not have been a people without the power of the Spirit at work. Along with a dozen others who help lead the Missional Wisdom Foundation, and the Epworth Project residents, the New Day lead teams, the faculty of the Academy for Missional Wisdom and all the other wonderful people who in some way participate in the unfolding of this adventure, we celebrate the emergence of God's work!

As we look to the coming years we believe that the Holy Spirit will show us more ways that the Missional Wisdom Foundation can help resource the historically mainline church for a vibrant future, drawing from our own roots as Methodists, Lutherans, Episcopalians, Presbyterians, American Baptists, and more. We believe that we can learn from the wisdom and best practices of the great Christian saints and mystics, and from modern reformers such as Dietrich Bonhoeffer, Dorothy Day, George MacLeod, Clarence Jordan, and John Perkins.

We believe that it is a new day for the church. We are not afraid or discouraged by the rapid cultural shifts in which we find ourselves, or the decline of what people have called the traditional church.[6] Instead, we look into the future with the firm conviction that God has wondrous plans for the church. We believe that God has initiated the pruning of the church that we now experience, so that we can be free of attachments that keep us from our missional vocation. We believe that our job is to live in a contemplative stance: to show up, pay attention, cooperate with God, and release the outcome.[7] If we will do that individually and communally, the church will thrive into a future alive with Christ.

For Reflection:

1. *Elaine and Larry shared their stories of how the Holy Spirit called them into the work they now do in the Missional Wisdom Foundation. How have you experienced the Holy Spirit calling you? Who are the companions God has brought into your journey?*

2. *What are some spiritual practices that could help ordinary Christians prepare to take risks in doing something new, as the Holy Spirit leads?*

6. What constitutes "traditional" when we look around the globe, for example, and through Christian history? There are many traditions at different times and places. What we must be about is the tradition behind the tradition, which is God's missional love reaching out through God's people to forgive, heal, reconcile, and make all things new.

7. These four steps—show up, pay attention, cooperate with God, and release the outcome—are my definition of a contemplative orientation. We discern where, when, and how to cooperate with God when we show up and pay attention! Our thought about this has been influenced partially by the teaching of Sister Marguerite Buchanan of the Mercy Center in Burlingame, California. Sister Marguerite describes much of the Christian life as being oriented toward showing up, paying attention, speaking the truth in love, and releasing the outcome.

2

Can Progressive Christians
Be Missional?

*In this chapter we will think about the theological underpinnings
for the ministry of evangelism, beginning with the acknowledge-
ment of destructive forms of mission and evangelism that have been
practiced in order to exploit and colonize people. We will think about
the resonance of healthy evangelism with the inclusive, nonviolent,
peacemaking commitments of progressive Christianity.*

PEOPLE ASK ME (ELAINE) sometimes why we use the term "missional wisdom," what it means and where it came from. I have
even been accused of not being Christian because the phrase
doesn't have the name of Christ in it. Really. The word *missional*
simply means "sent out." Missional ecclesiology is the fundamen-
tal Christian identity of the church being God's sent out people.
This identity is both communal and individual. We are, in the
words of Henri Nouwen, "taken, blessed, broken and given."[1] A

---

1. Henri Nouwen develops this fourfold meditation in his beautiful little
book, *Life of the Beloved.*

missional life is always a Eucharistic life. To take the bread and drink the cup is to say to God, "Here I am, Lord, send me."[2]

There are many definitions of wisdom but one of the best understandings I have received is that wisdom is knowledge gained through suffering. I learned this from Wendy Miller, my dear friend and gifted teacher of spiritual direction. I have also observed that the wisest people I've ever known are those who have suffered the most and whose ministry is with those who suffer.

So being people of missional wisdom means we are God's people, gathered, forgiven, healed, blessed, and distributed to participate in God's mission of healing and redeeming the cosmos. We go fully informed and listening to the knowledge gained through suffering, the knowledge that we receive from those among whom we are sent and the knowledge we ourselves bear as wounded healers.[3] In this era of postcolonialism and neocolonialism, the first voices we must deeply hear are those who have been harmed by exploitive, violent forms of Christendom. These are not simply historic voices. All around us there are living souls who cry out to be liberated from religiously framed violence, from exclusion, labeling, shaming, attacking, dehumanizing violence done blasphemously in the name of Jesus. We must heed what they say, and repent. Otherwise we cannot become the face of Jesus to our neighbors, nor will we recognize the face of Jesus in them.

Another way to put this is that missional wisdom is evangelism done in the name, spirit, and with the methods of Jesus. We have a lot of repenting to do, for the practice and motives for "evangelism" have become even more polluted than the poisoned theory and practice of "mission," if that were possible.

One of the saddest realities we must face as a church is the way that mission and evangelism have been hijacked to serve the interests of empire. By this I mean the church functioning in

2. Isaiah 6:8.

3. Henri Nouwen, in his classic meditation, *The Wounded Healer*, reminds us that if we do not attend to the healing of our wounds, we become wounded wounders. Becoming a healer is not automatic. It requires intentionality, a contemplative orientation, sometimes therapeutic and focused spiritual resources, and most of all, time.

collusion with secular and military power to dominate indigenous people and "others" of any kind in order to exploit and subjugate people and steal their resources. This has happened throughout much of Christian history.[4] We cannot faithfully bear witness to the real gospel as a church unless we come to terms with what has happened along these lines. We must actively work to heal the wounds caused by destructive, colonial, imperialistic forms of "mission" and "evangelism." That healing begins with our own repentance, moves into an awakened theological imagination, and continues to move outward in ever widening circles into a world torn apart by religious violence. So we must first take stock of the impact of exploitive forms of mission and evangelism, along with the real meanings of these words, then we will realize why progressive Christians are especially well suited for mission and evangelism in the manner of Jesus.

Again, the word *mission* simply means "sent out." Evangelism means "good messaging." Note: the root word in ev-*angel*-ism is "angel" or messenger. The question for us is, what kind of message are we sending about God simply by the way we live and who we are as people? Are we messengers, we sent out people, reflective of the life and teaching of Jesus? Do our neighbors encounter in us, day by day, a God whose meaning is love?

A History of Violence

As Larry and I began working on this book the world struggled to make sense of the September 11, 2012 murder of U.S. Ambassador to Libya, Chris Stevens, and three other Americans in the Embassy. The violent retaliation against the U.S. may have happened in part because of an anonymously created Youtube video crudely depicting demeaning images of the Prophet Mohammed. Extremists stormed the U.S. Embassy in Benghazi, Libya and unleashed a global wave of violence against Americans that spun out for weeks with more innocent people killed each day.

4. For more about the church and empire, see Rieger, *Christ and Empire*.

Today, less than a year later, the world was rocked by news of the slow beheading of Franciscan priest Father Francois Murad, by Syrian extremists due to his alleged collaboration with President Bashar Assad's regime. Men and boys looked on, jeering, filming the atrocity as Father Murad and two other people were murdered. The video was released onto the Internet in hopes of terrifying a watching world into compliance with extremist demands.[5]

Violence from radical Judaism against its neighbors is just as devastating. The invasion and brutal oppression of Palestine by Israel is a replication of the kind of violence Jews have suffered from others for millennia. The use of omnipresent military checkpoints that prevent Palestinian women from getting medical care during labor and delivery, that limit access to goods and services, and that in other ways dehumanize and terrorize Palestinians, is unconscionable. The fact that many Palestinians are Christian seems to make no difference to Zionist American Christians who enthusiastically support the Israeli colonization and destruction of Palestine.[6]

Within the United States perhaps the most blatant example of religious violence is the "witness" of Westboro Baptist Church as it spreads a gospel of hate and violence against multiple groups of "others" with whom it disagrees, particularly gays and lesbians. The website for Westboro Baptist Church is www.godhatesfags. com.

Most of the world, including the majority of devout Jews, Christians, and Muslims are appalled by religious violence. President Barak Obama, in his September 25, 2012 speech to the General Assembly of the United Nations, condemned the murder of Ambassador Stevens and his colleagues. Voicing the progressive Christian commitment of his denomination, the United Church of Christ, President Obama said:

5. www.nydailynews.com/new/world/short-syrian-terrorists-behead -catholic-priest-article-1.1387069.

6. For a profound and deeply reflective narrative of American attitudes to Israeli violence in Palestine and what the church needs to learn from Palestinians see Bush, *Learning from the Least.*

> Like me, the majority of Americans are Christian, and yet we do not ban blasphemy against our most sacred beliefs. Moreover, as President of our country, and Commander-in-Chief of our military, I accept that people are going to call me awful things every day, and I will always defend their right to do so. Americans have fought and died around the globe to protect the right of all people to express their views—even views that we disagree with.[7]

With the rise in religiously inspired terrorism, ongoing war in the Middle East, and the constant threat of nuclear and biological warfare, global political leaders like President Obama who also claim commitment to one of the three great Abrahamic religions, must now more than ever before devote themselves to a reduction in religious violence. The future of life on earth is at stake.

Religious leaders from all three faiths must help in this work of peace, for without us political leaders cannot get the job done. Will such peacemaking require us to compromise our faith or deny our commitment to our own religion? Historically the more conservative a group has been about orthodoxy, the more inclined it has been toward violence. (A notable exception to this is the Anabaptist tradition of nonviolence, found among Mennonites who are theologically conservative.)

Theologically progressive Christians believe it doesn't have to be this way. One can hold deeply cherished religious convictions and have loving, constructive relationships with those who do not. Many of us believe that working toward interreligious coexistence and friendship causes us to examine more deeply what we believe, and why. For the gospel to truly be for all people, it must be able to lovingly engage, not do violence toward all people. A gospel that cannot stand up under such commitments is scarcely the gospel of Jesus.

In a recent interview Hebrew Bible scholar Walter Brueggemann was asked what he believes is the greatest problem facing

---

7. http://www.guardian.co.uk/world/2012/sep/25/obama-un-general-assembly-transcript.

Christianity today. His response was in keeping with his progressive theological orientation:

> Probably an attempt to get free of its past that is marked by authoritarianism and a kind of tacit violence. I think that many, many people are alienated from the church's offer of the gospel because they have been wounded by the church. I think the church's abusiveness that's in the headlines today is simply a token of much of the wounding that the church has done. To reform or renew the church beyond that . . . It is not easy or obvious how to do that. But that is our ecclesial work, I think.
>
> And I think that the church has allied itself with much in our society that contradicts the gospel, and for the church to claim its freedom from that is very difficult. It means top-heavy institutionalism, and complex, expensive government structures, all of which depended on a kind of affluence that is not in the church's future in our society. To learn to get along without that surplus of resources, and to get a mindset for traveling light institutionally, is a huge challenge for all of us. Basically what that means, however we work it out, is that we have to travel light. We can't afford to travel any other way.[8]

Brueggemann is right. We have a lot of work to do to heal the wounds of church functioning as empire, and to prepare the church to serve as Jesus serves. The first place for us to begin with this work is to reclaim the beautiful meaning of evangelism.

A New Definition

To put this quite simply, evangelism is the invitation to discipleship, which is a call to holiness, and holiness is an incarnational immersion in the love of God. Love does not exploit, violate, manipulate, or try to make a profit from the beloved. Love pours itself

8.http://www.religionnews.com/blogs/jana-riess/redefining-retirement-a-conversation-with-walter-brueggemann.

out for the beloved. That is the meaning of Philippians 2:6–11, the great Kenotic Hymn.[9]

St. Paul, wanting to make sure the Corinthian church understood that being filled with the Spirit means being filled with divine love, wrote: "Love is patient, love is kind, it isn't jealous, it doesn't brag, it isn't arrogant, it isn't rude, it doesn't seek its own advantage, it isn't irritable, it doesn't keep a record of complaints, it isn't happy with injustice, but it is happy with the truth. Love puts up with all things, trusts in all things, hopes for all things, endures all things. Love never fails."[10] Becoming one with God's love and God's mission, which is the consequence of evangelism, is a process of receiving and learning to give the love of God revealed in Jesus.

Does this sound too simple? Not oriented enough toward right doctrine? It is the path of the great Christian mystics, saints and martyrs, people like Salvadoran Archbishop Oscar Romero, who was gunned down at the church on March 24, 1980. They have shown us the way. Julian of Norwich, one of the greatest Christian theologians and mystics of all time, wrote, "Love is God's meaning." This orientation of radical love is inclusive, nonviolent, healing, and transformative. It is prophetic and it makes absolute sense to progressive Christians.

I have been teaching the theory and practice of evangelism for nearly a decade at Southern Methodist University. I have had the privilege of companioning hundreds of students over the years as they grappled with the overwhelmingly violent image they were given of evangelism. "I don't want to shove religion down people's throats" many have said on the first day of class. "I can't stand the exclusion and threats of hell," lamented others. "I only took this class because I had to," wrote many as I invited their questions and fears on the first day of class.

9. *Kenosis* is a Greek word that means "self-emptying." In the Kenotic Hymn Jesus empties himself of privilege and status, taking the form of a servant in order to bring salvation to the world. This hymn is about the flipping of power in the economy of salvation. The word *Lord* is recast as a kenotic lordship when used as a name for God.

10. 1 Corinthians 13:4–8, CEB.

Imagine their surprise, the progressive students, the ones who don't believe in the hell of eternal fire and torture, the ones who have Muslim friends or are married to agnostics, the ones who are gay, ecumenical, questioning their faith, recovering from toxic church or just plain confused, when they discover a definition of evangelism rooted in the ancient tradition that focuses on love as God's meaning. Here is the definition that I give them:

Christian evangelism is the holistic process of initiation of persons into the reign of God revealed in Jesus Christ, empowered by the Holy Spirit, and anchored in the church for the transformation and healing of the world.[11]

Again and again my most progressive students have become the most ardent evangelists, once they have been freed from bad theology. Here, in a nutshell, is what they learned the first few weeks of class.

A Process of Initiation

The first thing is that evangelism is a *process of initiation* that requires friendship, time, and trust. It takes at least two years for the average person to move from having some questions or conscious thought about becoming a follower of Jesus, to actually become a follower. Sometimes it takes much longer than that, especially for people who have been judged, shamed, violated, or in other ways harmed by Christians. Most people need multiple encounters with the gospel from a variety of people in different situations before they are ready to embrace the rigors of Christian life.

How did Jesus evangelize? He *lived with* the disciples, calling people who were naturally at odds together into community. Ever so slowly they came to faith as they interacted with Jesus in

---

11. This is my definition of evangelism, which I use in academic and congregational contexts. I am indebted to Betty Jeavons, William Abraham, Julian of Norwich, Hans Urs von Balthasar, Henri Nouwen, Julia Foote, George Fox, and several others for helping me to develop this definition. More than just a statement about theology, this definition is also something of a rule of life for me, that I seek to enflesh. Some days I almost get it right.

everyday life and were disillusioned of their own bad theology. Ever so slowly they learned that women are human. Samaritans are human. Tax collectors are human. Even Roman centurions are human. Jesus shows us that evangelism is a process that takes much time and loving, committed, genuine friendships between people.

It is significant the early Christians were called people of "the way." Evangelism is a journeying-together process as we go along our way. As Diana Butler Bass explains in *Christianity after Religion*, people have to belong, have to be welcomed to walk with those who are on "the way" and see how Christians behave and practice behaving with them before they can actually love and trust God. This requires welcoming people to journey with us just as Jesus invited the disciples. Along the way we encounter life together, and we contextually evangelize by being good news, being good messengers who enflesh the love of God with our fellow travelers. Every day is a new adventure.

I am not talking about friendship evangelism. Genuine friendships are relationships *without* an agenda. "Friendship evangelism" is never really about friendship when it has a church growth agenda. We have to give that up. It just isn't the way of Jesus. What we do find in the Gospels is a Jesus who offers friendship to all sorts of people, some of whom decide to follow him.

Jesus is never worried about "church growth." He is patently not dazzled by crowds or impressed with religious programs and buildings. In the one case where his disciples rave about the beauty of the temple, Jesus offers a cryptic statement about the temple's destruction, foretelling his own death and resurrection and the temple's literal destruction in AD 70. Jesus just isn't into buildings. He is into people. Jesus's angry words and threats of hell are always reserved for religious leaders who use their religion to exploit and oppress vulnerable people.

Into the Reign of God Revealed in Jesus Christ

Evangelism is a process of initiation of persons *into the reign of God revealed in Jesus Christ.* The initiation is into relationship with, respect for, and loving trust in Jesus.

Jesus, who is "the icon of the unseen God" (Col 1:15), and who makes clear to us that love is God's meaning, is the inexhaustible definition of grace. He is grace incarnate. In Jesus, mercy always triumphs over judgment. As Hebrews tells us, he empathizes with all our struggle and pain for he has been tested in every way that we are. He is a great high priest, able to mediate the love of God to us when we sin, fail, and are lost.

This means that at the most basic level Jesus respects us. Why would Jesus invest so much effort and love, to the point of death, if he did not think we were amazing? Respect for others is woven into everything Jesus says and does.

Jesus reveals to us a God whose reign is eternal and infinite, the God who has a mission in the world, which is the healing of the cosmos, the making of all things new! To be a follower of Jesus is to believe in, to love and trust and throw one's lot in with the maker-of-all-things-new God. But how does God intend to make all things new? Jesus, God incarnate, shows us the way.

When Jesus was born the world encountered a revelation of God that no one, *no one* expected . . . the God who finds solidarity with all our suffering, the God who descends to hell to bring us out. The God of missional wisdom. That is God's method, Jesus shows us. Descending into hell, as the original version of the Apostle's Creed teaches.

Jesus first descended into hell when he was born in a cave allotted to animals, a space that smelled like shit. Jesus's mother was pregnant before she got married in a culture that stoned fornicating women. Oh, the hell that women endure in so many parts of the world! The hell of exploitation and damnation over gender, the hell of servitude, of trafficking, of female circumcision, of rape, of being forced to marry and bear children year after year, the hell of fistulas and miscarriages and infant mortality, the hell of maternal mortality. Jesus came into women's hell with Mary. The making of all things new begins with God coming into our hell.

Even in utero Jesus's life was at risk. He would belong to an oppressed and despised minority. He would talk with a Nazarene accent,[12] thus become the butt of jokes. "Could anything good come from Nazareth?" Nathaniel sniped.[13] Jesus's parents brought the poor people's offering to the temple when he was born. That was all they could afford. What does it mean to follow a God who chooses the identity of those whose lives are marked for suffering before they are even born, the God of despised minorities, of the working poor, of the catastrophically poor, of the uneducated? This is the question of evangelism. For to evangelize is to companion others into following *that* God.

While he was still a baby a pogrom broke out, an "ethnic cleansing" of Jewish boys that forced Joseph, Mary, and Jesus to flee for his life. What does it mean to love and serve the God who was a refugee? In due time Jesus and his family returned to Nazareth, once the coast was clear. There, Jesus lived such an obscure, unimpressive life growing up that everyone was shocked when he came into public ministry and had *authority*. Wasn't he the carpenter's son? Who the hell did he think he was to claim Isaiah 61 as his own?

Jesus smelled like sweat, had the calloused hands of a working man, spent his final years homeless, was profiled and arrested on trumped up charges, sentenced to die without a fair trial, was tortured to death at the city dump. He descended into hell, the God of the damned.

What does it mean for us to follow the God of the damned? To be a Christian means to live like that. To evangelize others is to companion them into that life, which means that we ourselves must be living that life.

12. Nazareth was considered a backward village with a notable dialect that elicited the same kind of negative stereotypes as Southern, rural accents do in the U.S.

13. John 1:46.

Empowered by the Holy Spirit

This is not possible without the indwelling, empowering Holy Spirit. She must keep pointing us to Jesus, keep filling us with her faith that love wins. She must gift us, call forth from us more courage, integrity, and perseverance than we knew we had. She must heal us of our bigotry, lead us into all truth, turn our failures and mistakes into wisdom. None of us can love as Jesus loves unless we are filled with the Holy Spirit. And this requires a day by day opening of ourselves to the love of God. It means we have to be born again, born of the Spirit.

It means we have to live in a contemplative stance.

To be a contemplative is to show up, pay attention, cooperate with God, and release the outcome.[14] It is an orientation that is both inward and outward, one that is both cause and result of an increasing integration and wholeness within. Richard Rohr has written of this stance with clarity and power in his book, *The Naked Now: Seeing as the Mystics See.*

Anchored in the Church

One of the great challenges we face today in the process of evangelism is to initiate persons into a faith that is anchored in God's church. This is a difficult task because North American ecclesiology has been so perverted by consumerism and individualism and empire. We are nearly apostate, we have wandered so far from the church that Jesus launched.

Initiating newly forming Christians in the ways we have already considered and anchoring them in the "one holy, catholic, apostolic church" requires that we catechize them into the history of missional church. In some ways this is an alternative history than has been standard for many years. Rather than being a history of schisms, popes, wars and white, male leadership, it is a

14. My definition partially comes from an idea presented by Sister Marguerite Buchanan of the Mercy Center, Burlingame, California, in a workshop on truth-telling, relationships, and justice.

history of courageous Christians of all ages and many racial and ethnic groups who have chosen to live as Jesus lives, often at great cost to themselves. It is a history of renewal in the church brought about by ordinary, unauthorized people like the Beguines, the Lollards, and nuns on the bus.[15] Diana Butler Bass's recent volume, *A People's History of Christianity: The Other Side of the Story* is an excellent place to begin.[16]

This part of initiation includes a generous, informed, and appreciative awareness of multiple Christian traditions. We never do new Christians a favor by giving them the idea that our little congregation and tradition is superior to all others, or that we are right and everyone else is wrong. Jesus consistently poked holes in his followers' special doctrinal and political balloons. We must let him also poke holes in ours.

Yet we do need to help our emerging followers of Jesus learn about the history and missional DNA of our local congregation and our theological branch on the family tree, for they are going to be formed in practices of prayer, hospitality, and justice in our specific story.

The very best way for us to initiate others into healthy communal life as the church is for us to model it. Jesus found this a daunting task. His disciples constantly jockeyed for power, wanted to incinerate others who disagreed with them, wanted to stop others outside their circles from using Jesus's name, wanted to manipulate Jesus into favoritism and cronyism. Every day Jesus seemingly faced a new set of idiotic questions and behavior from his would be church. And yet he soldiered on. He respected them enough to do that.

And so must we.

15. http://www.networklobby.org/bus
16. Bass, *A People's History of Christianity.*

For the Transformation and Healing of the World

So as we invite, companion, welcome and initiate others into this holy life, we have to help each other remember that the missional God we love—the triune, kenotic, making-all-things-new God—is determined to heal the cosmos. As N. T. Wright has so beautifully described in *Surprised by Hope*, we get to participate in that healing. We get to help bring about the redemption of all things, the mighty uncursing of the world. This is a theology of evangelism—missional wisdom—that makes a compelling case for all Christians, not just progressives. But enough of talking about the theory. It's time to get to some stories of transformation.

For Reflection:

1. *When you think about following the God who is revealed in Jesus, what attracts you? What challenges you? Why?*

2. *Where have you experienced missional wisdom as defined in this chapter? How did it impact your life?*

3. *What are some ways, in your context, that you could personally be involved in healing the wounds of Christendom?*

3

What is New Monasticism in a Progressive Mainline Tradition?

In this chapter we will focus on understanding what new monasticism is, how it relates to the traditional church, and why it is important.

FOR THOSE OF US who focus our ministry on the development of missional communities, the term "new monasticism" is a real pain in the neck. It is a very precise and appropriate term, but because most people don't really think about monasticism at all, the distinction between "new monasticism" and "old monasticism" is lost on them. On top of that, the word itself sounds funny—people want to know if you are saying "numismaticism," which is the practice of collecting coins. When they finally realize you are talking about monasticism, they very often lapse into visions of balding men with funny haircuts in weird robes, whipping themselves and chanting "Bring out your dead."[1]

---

1. With a tip of the hat to the classic film *Monty Python and the Holy Grail* (1975).

Yet the term lingers because it is both precise and accurate. New monasticism is really all about being a new kind of monk in the twenty-first century, a person who chooses to live in a Christian community with a focus on service, especially with the poor and marginalized. It is "new" because people are reimagining what it means to be "in community," and are shedding some of the historical restrictions like celibacy (many new monastic folk are married) and lifelong vows. They are capturing the ancient prophetic role of monastic communities in a way that complements both historic monasticism and the traditional church.

In a recent edition of the Center for Action and Contemplations' quarterly newsletter "The Mendicant," Richard Rohr describes the "alternative orthodoxy" of the Franciscan Order (which dates back to the twelfth century) in a wonderful and enlightening way:

> The Franciscan School was normally a minority position inside of the Catholic and Christian tradition, but one that was never condemned or considered heterodox. Instead, it emphasized different issues, behaviors, and perspectives, and placed its attention on the immense and universal implications of the Incarnation of God in Christ. Franciscanism was, in effect, a parachurch viewpoint on the edge of the inside of organized Christianity.
> The starting place for Franciscanism was suffering instead of sinfulness, its Christ was also cosmic instead of just personal, and its primary church was creation itself. It preferred the bottom to the top. It emphasized inclusion of the seeming outsider over the inside group and mysticism over mere morality. Its prophecy was lifestyle in itself, and even poverty was preferred to private perfection, because Jesus, "the image of the invisible God" (Colossians 1:15), was himself humble and poor. Its genius was that it found a way to incorporate, include, and embrace what others called a disadvantage (2 Corinthians 12:10 and Philippians 3:7).[2]

---

2. Rohr, "The Franciscan Alternative Orthodoxy," 1.

In describing the points of focus of the "old" monastic community he loves, Rohr helps us to focus on the ideals that "new" monasticism strives for too. A position that is faithful to God the Creator, empowered by the Spirit, and deeply informed by the Incarnation of Christ. A vantage point on the "edge of the inside." A focus on suffering, not sin; the bottom instead of the top; simplicity rather than excess. A life lived in the expectation that the Holy Spirit is an active and vital participant in the lives of all rather than a scowling referee poised to throw the yellow flag.

And as the new monastic works to redefine her life and her relationships into this deeply held orientation of loving God and loving others, she does not do so at the cost of abandoning the church. Instead, she speaks into the church, inviting all to join her in service and humility. Throughout the centuries, monks have called the larger church to reform and to repent—Dominic, Francis, Luther, Rohr—but they have done so from within. The new monastic calls the church back to a life and an order that lives in the way that Christ lives by presenting a real-life example of that love and way of life.

Much of the remainder of this book examines the details of establishing and living in new monastic communities, but before we get to that, we should dwell for a moment on our motivations. Why should we live as new monastics? Is there something special about a rule of life, or a focus on serving, or on embracing the reality of God's action in the world that leads to spiritual growth in a way that other spiritual practices do not?

Yes and no. One of the concepts that gets a lot of discussion in many of the forums we read and participate in is the idea of "non-dualistic" thinking. One of the influences that many of us in the Western world have picked up from our Greco-Roman and Enlightenment roots is the inclination to see things as mutually exclusive polar opposites. Black or white, good or evil, right or wrong. Non-dualistic thinking would ask us to reject that artificial distinction and instead to imagine a position where many ideas have ranges of outcomes or implications. There may in fact be many good answers instead of just one—and, embracing that idea, we believe that new monasticism is one good answer to the question of how to live a Christian life. Not the only good answer, not the one true way, but one wonderful path that many follow to grow closer to God.

Stories of Our Life Together

Members of the communities we are part of tell us that regularly praying together transforms the way they look at prayer and each other. Praying frequently and deeply with a small, consistent group of people is a very intimate experience, one that is very different from the community prayer in a traditional church service or Sunday school class. When people pray together over time, the fruits of prayer become apparent and new monastics report seeing changes in themselves and in their companions as prayers are answered and deeper issues arise. Adam from the Bonhoeffer House puts it this way: community prayer "exposes the vulnerability in our lives and I think it allows our vulnerability to come out when it otherwise would not. It's a very safe place and we are accountable to one another to respect that vulnerability."[3]

Community prayer also broadens the scope of prayer for many. Amy from the Romero House explains that praying together changes how deeply she cares for the people she lives with and that it changes the focus of the prayers. "When I am hearing petitions from other people, I am being reminded to pray for other people in the community and for other events that are going on that I may or may not remember in my own individual prayer." Brandon and George of the Bonhoeffer House recall a time when their prayer life was transformed in the act of praying together over a troubled neighbor who stopped by the house for prayer. Together, George and Brandon prayed over the man, growing increasingly fervent and inspired. When they stopped, the man looked up and asked

3. The quotations from community members included in the rest of this chapter are taken from a series of interviews conducted by Larry Duggins in January and February 2012. We have included their comments with their permission.

them to continue! They took out their copy of *Common Prayer*,[4] and, as George described, "We were literally going from day to day in that liturgy for about two hours, reading the liturgy and praying! That moment . . . you could tell we were all visually, physically, emotionally right there in the Kingdom of God. The Kingdom of God was very near right then."

Community prayer plays an important role in fostering an environment of support and nurture among the community members. Katie from the Palmer House explains that in her opinion, it is the prayer and accountability to one another that separates new monastic living from a typical roommate situation. "We are in Christian community," she says, "so we can build one another up in our Christian walk and faith."

Living in community fosters changes in the way that people understand hospitality. Rachel from the Romero House grew up in an environment of hospitality that was redefined for her through her time in community. "My mom always taught me how to be hospitable. When it became part of my Rule of Life . . . it came from a different place. I'm not hospitable because my mom says that is what a Southern lady does—I am hospitable because I feel like that is what God is calling me to do." Her housemate Sarah emphasizes the importance of being deliberately hospitable. "I know for me, the intentionality is a big part of it. I did some of these things [in the past], but I am much more intentional now that I have committed to this Rule of Life and I know that we are all in it together."

The women of the Palmer House strongly believe in the power of potluck dinners. They see that form of hospitality as extending the comfort of home to their neighbors and to all who can come, and they see it as a witness for others to enter into a place that is dedicated to life focused on God and others. The opportunity for positive witness about living simply arises in the community potluck dinners. Luci from the Palmer House mentioned that she was always finding that people had strange misconceptions about living

4. *Common Prayer* is a wonderful prayer resource we use in all of our communities. See Claiborne, Wilson-Hartgrove, and Okoro, *Common Prayer*.

in community. She got questions about dress code and whether televisions were allowed, and she found that simply opening the house in a potluck helped to alleviate those. "I think hospitality helps," she said, "because everyone can see it!" Hospitality requires freely sharing, which in turn reinforces a deeper understanding of the "theology of enough."

Our rule of life, which we will discuss in more detail in a later chapter, calls for being aware of the power of possessions and for the fostering of the habit of living in sufficiency, not in excess. We call this the "theology of enough," and we find that living in community drives transformation in many with regard to possessions. George was driven to give away many of his possessions, including his books and his electronics. Jonathan was convicted when he realized that "even if I took away 90 percent of my stuff, I'd still be better off than a majority of the world." Luci was shocked when she was rejected for financial aid for college because they did not believe that she lived on so little. "It's just that I never thought of myself as poor," she said, "because I have everything I need."

One of my (Larry) very favorite stories of new monastic life and the "theology of enough" came out of an encounter with the Romero House. In one of my meetings with them, I asked about sources of conflict within the community. The residents were all very gracious and denied that there was any conflict, but I sensed that there was something unsaid. Finally, after much patience and prodding, one of them finally said, "Well, it's the refrigerator . . ." It turns out that the standard refrigerator was too small for them all to buy groceries for the week, and they were resorting to draconian planning and allocation schemes to have the refrigerated items on hand for specific events they had planned. I smiled, and came back the following week with an additional refrigerator someone had donated.

About a week later, I got another call from the Romero House asking me to come mediate a dispute. As I walked into the house, I saw the new refrigerator sitting in the corner of the dining room, unplugged. It turns out that the residents were struggling with the "luxury" of the second refrigerator, debating among themselves whether incurring the additional costs and energy consumption was justified under the "theology of enough." I was so proud of them I almost burst. Thus is the nature of community life!

The "theology of enough" is quite counter-cultural and represents an opportunity to share an example of living in a Christ-like way to those outside of the community. Amy of the Seymour House told how surprised her church congregation was when Clay and Errinne, residents of the Seymour House who were expecting their first child, turned down a kind offer for a baby shower. "They said, 'We've got enough. We don't need anymore.' In this day and age, people are usually wanting more than they need."

The Argument for New Monasticism

There are literally hundreds of these stories, but by now we hope that you can see the thread that connects them. Living as a new monastic is all about living as Jesus lived. It is about practicing what we believe in daily life, and it is about maintaining a steady focus on God and on others.

A quick scan of any of the Gospels confirms this way of living. Jesus lived, worked and worshiped with a small group of followers. They regularly took time to pray, both together and individually. They talked about the big issues—the coming of the Kingdom of God, the role of religion in daily life—but they did so while the were out in the world helping the poor, the weak, and the marginalized. They lived simply, and they relied on God to lead them and to provide for them. They exercised radical hospitality, and found many opportunities to eat and drink with those who were outcasts and marginalized. They held each other up, learned from each other, and grew together as God used them to transform the world.

That is the goal of new monastic life.

For Reflection:

1. *How is new monastic life different from being active in a traditional church? Are the two mutually exclusive?*

2. *What are the risks and pitfalls of living together in community?*

3. *Does our culture encourage people to live in this way?*

4

Is This a Hostile Takeover
of the Church?

In this chapter we will focus on the most constructive and loving way to navigate the tension between attractional and missional ecclesiology so that the church can get ready to anchor missional and new monastic communities.

THE MAN, WHOM I (Elaine) will call "Frank" looked at me, worry lines creasing his forehead. "But if we prepare and deploy the Christians inside the church to leave the building and programs and do ministry in their neighborhoods," he sputtered, "who will be left in the church? We won't have a church any more!"

"What do you mean by 'church?'" I responded, knowing what the answer would be. I was at a conference for evangelism and discipleship ministries and had given a presentation on creating missional communities in our neighborhoods.

Frank was unhappy. He did not like my question. "Well, everyone knows the church is about people, but my church has a beautiful sanctuary and a first-rate organist, and you should see the stained glass windows. But never mind that. If we send people out to do church in other places, who is going to pay for the programs and building?" Frank shrugged his shoulders miserably. "I hate to say things like that. It sounds like I'm after people's money, and really what I just want is for the church to grow and be alive like it used to be."

Frank was well intentioned and truly wanted to do what was right, but he was unable to imagine a both/and church, or a different kind of attractional church. As he listened to me talk about missional ecclesiology he felt like it was a hostile takeover of the "real" church. What Frank thought of as the real, "normal" church is what Alan Hirsch, Alan Roxburgh, Michael Frost and others have called the "attractional church."[1] When you look at this model objectively, it doesn't take long to realize that it is alien to how Jesus lived and what he taught. It is not at all like the apostolic communities of the New Testament.

An attractional church is one that is centered on attracting people into the church building and programs, with the worship gathering being the centerpiece and most important activity of the week. In an attractional church the assumption is that discipleship happens when people are faithful participants in programs that take place in the church building. Ministry is led by professionals. It is important to make the church as likeable as possible so that as many outsiders as possible will come in. So the musicians need to be excellent, the preacher a dynamic speaker who can connect with people emotionally, and the children's ministry entertaining and informative. The "seeker" churches that became very popular in the 1990s were premier examples of the attractional church.

The church growth movement of the 1980s and 1990s was overwhelmingly oriented toward planting attractional churches, and in most denominations and non-denominational groups, this has been the dominant model of church for the past century in North America. We have been told that it is the "traditional" form of church. However, this kind of ecclesiology is recent and is rooted in market capitalism, with core values of getting a corner on

1. For his basic approach to missional ecclesiology as the forgotten ways of the gospel see Hirsch, *The Forgotten Ways*.

the market, undercutting the competition, anticipating the trends among consumers, and remembering the bottom line. This is a consumer-driven church, where people come to a special building with its menus of options in exactly the same way they go to an upscale shopping center to buy goods and services, have an eating experience, and see a movie. Instead of the driver being the Holy Spirit's call into the rigors of partnership with God in the world, the consumer of religious products calls the shots.

The part of the attractional model that is a problem is not that it attracts people to church. Lord knows, Jesus wants people in the church. But it has to do with *why* people are attracted, *how* they are attracted, and *what* we are attracting them *to*. At the core it has to do with what we mean by "church."

"Attractional" could mean something altogether different.

A Jesus-like church that is missional *is* attractive to people who want to experience God and help bring about transformation of a broken world. It is very attractive to people who believe the church should be radically inclusive, a healing place, and a place where people figure out their unique call in life so that they can live missionally in their neighborhood. It is attractive to the same kind of motley crew today that was attracted into the original church on the day of Pentecost. There were 120 men and women gathered together, filled with the Holy Spirit and sent out to change the world. The space they were in was borrowed and mostly irrelevant, an anonymous upper room. The attraction was all about God and people in relationship, on mission with good news.

So how can we help people like Frank and his church develop a missional imagination and become dissatisfied with consumer church? This is not an easy task. Sometimes nothing will make a stuck church or a stuck leader budge. In some cases you simply have to let them be and go on and invest your time and energy where there is openness. This is really what Jesus meant when he said to shake the dust off our feet when we who bring the news of the Kingdom of God are not welcomed. He meant shake off the dust of inhospitality and non-receptivity, offer a prayer for the folks who just don't "get it," and move on. There will be others who will hear the word with gladness. This teaching also means we are never to do hostile takeovers, except for that bit about breaking down the gates of hell.

What is most helpful is to show Frank and his friends examples of what you are talking about. Take them on some field trips or immersions. Let them see and hear real missional communities, healthy new monastic communities, and strong both/ and churches.[2] Let them ask questions and surface their fears and worries with people who have figured out how to be missional. There is nothing better than seeing the real thing. And the truth is, only about 3 percent of people are able to hear someone else cast a vision either orally or in written form, and really understand it. The other 97 percent need to see an example.

Once Frank and his friends have seen some real examples and have been able to ask questions of the people who are engaged in missional ecclesiology, the crack in the foundation of attractional ecclesiology will open just a bit. At that point introduce a short term study of missional ecclesiology, making it fun and interesting. Begin to dream with them about what it might mean for a formerly attractional, consumer church to turn a corner and become an anchor church. Help them understand that dualistic, either/or thinking will only keep us stuck and polarized. Invite them to imagine the solution to the dilemma.

Meanwhile, keep giving them opportunities to meet, read, listen to, watch or visit people who are fully engaged in missional ecclesiology, on the ground. There is something about living as Jesus lives, loving as Jesus loves, that is wildly contagious. It doesn't take long for fake church to lose its appeal. For the people who continue to resist and disparage the vision that you are casting, let them go. Even Jesus let the rich young man go when he realized what it would mean to really follow Jesus. Jesus was sad about the

2. By "both/and churches" I mean churches that have moved from being consumer congregations, to anchor churches that are attracting people to follow the real Jesus and live lives that honor the Jesus of the Gospels. These churches are anchors to all sorts of missional micro-communities out in the neighborhoods of their members. That is the right kind of "attractional" church, one that truly honors God revealed in Christ.

man, not because he missed a whopper of a "giving unit,"[3] but because the man was blinded by his own resources to the abundance of life Jesus came to give.

Alan Roxburgh and Scott Boren say that along with exposing the congregation to good paradigms, begin to introduce experiments around the edge of church life. In the last section of *Introducing the Missional Church* they lay out a step by step plan for helping a congregation, especially its clergy and lay leadership, to become educated about missional ecclesiology and to engage in experiments so that it can change. Once about 20 percent of the active population of the church is engaged in missional experiments, they state, the church reaches a tipping point so that it is ready to fully become an anchor to missional communities.

The sad fact is that many attractional churches are simply not willing to change, even though they know they are in trouble. My friend Beth Crissman started a ministry ten years ago called Plowpoint, to help churches get ready for change. Beth told me that she realized that inevitably, stuck churches are stuck and declining because people have forgotten how to treat one another well. As an expert in behavioral change, Beth developed a method of working with congregations to help members determine where they need to learn to behave in more loving ways with each other. Once the church has learned anew how to love one another (the most basic command of Jesus), they are ready to become missional. For the past decade she and her team have helped hundreds of congregations "break ground for the seed of the gospel."[4] Beth says that sometimes churches think they want help but when they find out what it will require in terms of repentance—acknowledging where they have gone astray and turning and going in the right direction—they say "No thanks, that is going to be too hard." In those cases, it is best to let them be. Shake off the dust and pray. Do not try a hostile takeover.

3. One of the ways that we betray our exploitive orientation in the church is our use of the term "giving units" to refer to people made in the image of God.

4. For more on this extraordinary ministry see www.plowpoint.org.

I am deeply convinced that the larger, vibrant churches of the future, the ones that will still have buildings and paid staff, will not resemble the attractional/consumer churches of today. There will be far fewer of them, for one thing. But more importantly, they will carry a different DNA. They will be anchors for all kinds of missional communities and initiatives in theological education for lay people. There will be large worship celebrations, to be sure, with great preaching and music and liturgy. But that won't be seen as the most important thing that happens in the church. Instead, the defining characteristic of the church will be its ability to equip and deploy ordinary Christians into the world, where they will cultivate real disciples and form alternative communities that provide a foretaste of heaven. This work will not be done to make a financial profit in the anchor church. It will be done in order to cooperate with God in the mission of making all things new.

In the chapter "Preparing the Congregation to Anchor a Missional Church" you will find much more detailed information for helping a church that is ready, to launch missional and new monastic communities. Moving forward, let us pray for God's church everywhere, for the courage and persistence we need to become attractive for the right reasons and in the missional way, and for a deep unwillingness to do hostile takeovers in the name of Jesus.

For Reflection:

1. *What must we give up and what must we take up to help our attractional churches become truly missional?*

2. *How can we help the "Franks" in our lives know that this is not a hostile takeover, but the movement of the Holy Spirit?*

3. *How can we best support the spiritual pioneers and innovators in our denomination who are opening our missional imagination?*

5

Theological Education for a Missional Church

Theological education, in tandem with the church, has to adapt quickly to the need for leadership development for new paradigm ministry. In this chapter we will survey some of the ways that clergy and laity can be equipped for missional and new monastic ministry, and how judicatory leaders have the power to open the way, encourage, and protect the emerging communities and their leaders.

WITHIN A YEAR OF launching New Day and the Epworth Project, while we were still very new at finding our way forward with the rule of life and discerning our missional context, word leaked out to the public. People began to call, email, and simply show up, curious about what we were doing. Were we an emerging church? Were we hippies? Were we a cult? We received all kinds of questions, mostly friendly. We told inquirers that we were like partially formed gelatin, still kind of wobbly and fragile, but they were welcome to come and be with us if they didn't mind that. So they came.

About three years into our formation a group of persons from New Mexico and West Texas, and another group from Oklahoma, unknown to each other, contacted us at the same time, requesting an immersion weekend with our communities. By that time we had three monastic houses and two New Day communities, and several other signs of emerging life around the Metroplex. So we welcomed them and put together what we now affectionately call the Spontaneous Combustion Immersion. We decided to invite our guests to sleep at the monastic houses, even if that meant on sofas or the floor, even if they stayed with people who didn't speak English. They happily agreed. It would be a full immersion.

Over a span of two and a half days we sojourned with our guests at all our communities, interviewing residents, noting how the Epworth Houses and the New Day communities were contextualizing their ministry among immigrants, latchkey children, and homeless people. It was a regular pilgrimage. We traveled to DeSoto, Texas, south of Dallas, where our friends John and Teresa Musser had started a missional demonstration micro-farm called Aquaponics and Earth.[1] Our immersion friends learned the Musser's story, how they had been traveling evangelists for decades, and how God called them to develop a missional micro-farm because, said the Holy Spirit, teaching others to become sustainable through locally grown food would be the way to do missions in the future. No longer could the Mussers go on preaching crusades as they had done in the past. Now their task was to go in the name of Jesus and offer slow food companionship to impoverished orphanages and villages, helping them to build tilapia tanks and aquaponic systems for growing fresh, nutritious food year round.

Neither John nor Teresa had ever raised so much as a radish. They had to teach themselves using Youtube and visits to the Walt Disney Epcot Center where they learned how to farm fish. They had been at it for a couple of years when we showed up with our immersion friends. The shocking abundance of their garden and fish tanks mesmerized everyone. Our west Texas guests, coming from the drought ravaged and economically depressed Panhandle,

---

1. See http://www.aquaponicsandearth.org.

quickly realized how transformational an agricultural missional community like this could be in their corner of the world. Imaginations opened wide to new possibilities.

In between field trips we spent time at Adrian House, where we offered classes in biblical and theological foundations for this form of ministry. Our guests were diverse, from the west Texas rancher to a school board member, two denominational judicatory leaders from Oklahoma, a handful of clergy, and ordinary church members. By the end of the immersion we all realized that something profound had just happened, beyond our immediate experience. We were being called into the work of new forms of theological education far beyond what we already offered contextually to students in the Epworth Project. The Spontaneous Combustion Immersion lit a fire that now burns coast to coast.

Over the next several months increasing numbers of people came to spend time with us. We always made space for them in one or more of our monastic houses, just as we had done with the first immersion. The people living in the houses realized as never before that a ministry of hospitality is often inconvenient. It wasn't easy for students to welcome pilgrims during midterm week. But more importantly they learned that in the stranger we meet Christ.

Meanwhile I (Elaine) began to receive many invitations to speak across the United States, telling the story of what was happening with New Day and the Epworth Project. I met with a group of non-instrumental Church of Christ elders who wanted to plant missional communities in military housing, a group of gay men in Houston who were already doing good work with homeless teens and wanted to create a residential community, and groups of bishops, clergy, and laity who wanted to find a way forward in the face of church decline. I talked to liberals, conservatives, postmoderns, senior citizens, vegans, and at least one anarchist. Everywhere I went, the more I shared with people, the hungrier they were to learn how to do this kind of ministry. My friend Dr. Rebekah Miles said in her Arkansas drawl, "Elaine, you've become an itinerant evangelist, but not like any I ever saw."

Again and again at the close of speaking events, pastors came to me with tears in their eyes saying, "I was going to leave ministry. I had decided I couldn't take it any more. The way we do church no longer makes sense to me. For my own sanity I decided I had to get out. But today you have given me hope. I want to learn how to do what you are doing in Dallas. That is what my heart longs to do. Where do I start? *They didn't teach us how to do this in seminary.*"

Right around then *Longing for Spring* was published, a book I had written with my friend and colleague Scott T. Kisker. It was our "Ninety-five theses"[2] nailed to the door of a declining United Methodist Church, urging all of us to pay attention to how Methodism began. Early Methodism was very much like a lay monastic movement, we argued, with a rule of life, small, missional communities of lay people, and a preference for working among populations ignored by the church. The church is not a club and not a business, we said. It is the living body of Christ on earth. It is time for us to return to our first love and our missional vocation.

In the book we presented a brief history of monastic renewal in the church, told our personal stories, and cast a vision for a new day for the church. We discussed ways that new monastic and missional community formation could emerge within the UMC using the already existing polity and structures of the denomination, everything from the ordination process to the use of closed churches and camps for monastic communities. The existing church could welcome and facilitate emergence and benefit from it, we argued. Renewal could happen in this way. I told the story of our fledgling work in Texas. We included in the book a six-week study guide so

2. Tradition says that on October 31, 1517, All Saints Day, Martin Luther nailed a document called the "Ninety-five Theses" to the door of the castle church in Wittenberg, Germany. His document protested what he regarded as corruption in the church, especially around the practice of "indulgences." He called the church to fidelity and integrity. This event is considered the spark that led to the Protestant Reformation. However, there were many people in addition to Luther who led multiple strands of reformations, including Menno Simons and the Anabaptists. For a great resource on the many strands of reformation that erupted in the sixteenth century see Matheson, ed., *Reformation Christianity*. For a quick review of Luther and the Ninety-five theses see http://en.wikipedia.org/wiki/The_Ninety-Five_Theses.

that small groups could use it to move into discernment and the initial stages of community formation. I began taking stacks of this book to speaking engagements.

Some bishops and other judicatory leaders started asking their cabinets and clergy to read *Longing for Spring* along with *The Mystic Way of Evangelism*,[3] which cast a vision for a new understanding of faith sharing that is grounded in a contemplative stance and steeped in the wisdom of the saints and mystics. Both books advance the position that real evangelism is never coercive, violent, manipulative, exploitive, or about making a profit. On the contrary, it is kenotic, giving life, and is a way of life that invites others through relationship and presence. In short it is the way of holiness. This kind of evangelism, I argued, is faith sharing carried out in the spirit and manner of Jesus. Both books describe dreams for new forms of theological education that are more like Outward Bound[4] than a university classroom.

A radical shift in how we prepare leaders is necessary and soon, or seminaries will not survive the culture shift. Most of the way we prepared people for church leadership in the past 150 years is simply out of touch with political, economic, social, and religious realities of our culture.

Some of my students and clergy friends who read about different forms of theological education in *The Mystic Way of Evangelism* said, "My God. This is what we hoped to do when we came to seminary. We wanted to learn to pray, to hear the Holy Spirit, to live a contemplative life, to know how to transform broken communities and form disciples along the way. But in seminary we don't have time for any of that. We have so many books to read and papers to write, so much pressure to perform or we will lose our scholarships. We can't afford to lose our scholarships because seminary is so expensive." They told me about their $50,000 student loan debt for seminary and how they would not be able to innovate in the church or serve bi-vocationally because they had to

3. Heath, *The Mystic Way of Evangelism*.

4. Outward Bound is a wilderness survival program that develops strong leadership and team-building skills. See http://www.outwardbound.org.

work fulltime for the established church in order to pay off student loans. Maybe thirty years into the future when loans were paid and their children grown and gone they would have the financial ability to take risks in how they led the church, but not now, even though they wanted to. This is what they said.

The more I travel, though, and listen to church leaders from mainline denominations, the more I find a deep desire to retool for a better future, one in which the church leaves its fortressed walls and internally focused programs and truly embodies John Wesley's maxim, "The world is my parish." Pastors and others seem open to new forms of theological education. What is most hopeful to many judicatory leaders seems to be the possibility that new forms of community might be fostered while continuing to tend existing congregations, and new forms of theological education could emerge from the old for institutions that want to continue the mission of equipping fruitful Christian leaders. A both/and approach can be used. A hostile takeover is unnecessary. There is no need to crucify the declining models of church and seminary. Love can be the practice as we live into God's future together.

The Academy for Missional Wisdom

By 2011 so many people had asked so many questions and had so much desire to learn to start missional communities and new monastic houses, we knew the time had come to start the Academy for Missional Wisdom. As has been the case with everything else, we found our way forward by trial and error. We asked the first two cohorts to serve as pilot groups and assured them we would make mistakes large and small, and would need their feedback to help us be a better training program in the future. Some two dozen brave souls agreed to pilot the first iteration of the Academy.

Today there are AMW cohorts from coast to coast. The Academy is not a full curriculum of theological education. It focuses on a deep understanding of missional ecclesiology, equipping laity and clergy with theological foundations, and practical skills to start missional and new monastic communities. We are still learning how to do this, as every cohort is locally contextualized. It has taken a lot of work and thought to develop a hybrid model of theological education[5] that combines immersion experiences, training retreats, spiritual direction, online classes, practicums and coaching, and delivers it all in the learners' context.

From a logistics perspective we had to figure out how to provide an excellent learning experience for a minimal cost, and how to work with denominational leaders and existing institutional structures to support the training of laity for this kind of ministry. We had to find the right software that is the most user-friendly, and learn the best methods for online instruction. We sought grants and donations to cover the costs that tuition could not cover.

Each year we get better at it. When we make mistakes we always say, "Failure is our best friend. We gain wisdom through failure. We are failing our way forward." This is a philosophy we teach everyone who journeys with us, because the first thing we have to contend with when we begin to pioneer new forms of ministry is our profound fear of failure in the church.[6]

We are now designing a judicatory leaders track so that bishops, area ministers, presbyters, superintendents and others who preside over multiple clergy and congregations can understand the theological foundations of missional ecclesiology and can help to create a hospitable environment for such ministry to flourish in their jurisdictions. We have spent considerable effort shaping the training of clergy in order to open the path in their congregations for laity to engage this work.

This winter we will launch our first Youth Academy for Missional Wisdom, in response to a group of junior high and high school girls in North Carolina who asked if they could also be trained in this way. (How could we say no to that?) We are also designing series of Day Apart retreats for clergy who wish to begin to retool for missional ecclesiology and kenotic spirituality. Basically

---

5. Hybrid learning models that combine action/reflection contextualized learning, immersion experiences, mentoring, and online education with a "flipped classroom" are by far the most effective way to teach.

6. Chapter 6 in this book focuses on the gift of failure.

we try to go wherever we are invited to share our story and encourage others to follow the Holy Spirit into the new day. We are glad to innovate, experiment, and evaluate new forms of theological education that can help the church at large.

The Summer Immersion in Missional and New Monastic Life: A Way to Resouce Multiple Seminaries

My original inspiration for the summer immersion was a doctor of ministry class that I (Elaine) taught many years ago as part of a backpacking trip. Our focus for the class was formational community development. I knew that nothing would help us create a community faster than going on a challenging adventure together, one that involved the threat of bears, elemental needs, and plenty of hard work. So we literally went on a journey, and in the process our lives were changed. It was the most rewarding class I had ever taught up to that time. I began to think that seminary in general needed to be more like Outward Bound and less like a philosophy class.[7]

Then a few years ago I heard about a program called the Oregon Extension.[8] This interdisciplinary undergraduate program has been going strong for thirty-some years on top of a mountain in southern Oregon. Over a dozen Christian liberal arts colleges work together in a consortium, sending students to study for one semester while living in intentional community, engaging theology, issues of social and environmental justice, and learning with faculty who become mentors and friends. A visit to the Oregon Extension was a powerful confirmation of my conviction that new forms of theological education that enable students and faculty to

---

7. I have nothing against philosophy, mind you, it's just that I object to the way that philosophy has dominated theology in the Western church. Systematic theology is considered the "twin discipline" of philosophy. Theology should emerge from prayer and the Christian community's experience of God.

8. See http://oregonextension.org/.

live and work together as well as study, are going to be necessary in the years ahead.

My dream in designing the Summer Immersion was that it would spark lifelong friendships among participants, generate fruitful dialogue and a deeply missional imagination in all who took part, and that it would lead to a permanent program with multiple sites around the U.S. I envisioned eventually linking it to one or more of the participating divinity schools for purposes of accreditation of the courses, but for it to be a collaborative effort open to a wide array of seminaries.

More than anything I hoped the Summer Immersion would help us reimagine wineskins for theological education by creatively bringing together judicatory leadership, local churches, non-profits, students from multiple seminaries, and faculty from different seminaries and disciplines.

In the summer of 2013 this dream became reality when we launched the pilot of the Summer Immersion. This program was generously supported by the Fund for Theological Education. Five divinity students and one sociology student came to Asheville, North Carolina, where we then lived in intentional community following monastic rhythms of life for seven weeks. Four mornings per week we had classes (one on evangelism and the other on doctrine) then on Wednesdays students (and usually faculty) worked all day at Haywood Street Church, an innovative urban ministry that brings people without homes together with everyone else for a community meal, worship, and opportunities to work in the garden, receive acupuncture or massage, and enjoy a host of other options.[9] Housing for the students was at the Brooks Howell Home for retired missionaries and deaconesses. Thus the students' context for living was a community of seniors, some of whom were busy justice activists, some of whom were wheelchair bound and suffered dementia. Sharing meals, chapel, and conversations day to day on a senior campus was another form of learning.

The students went with the professors to visit, participate in, and learn from various rural ministries that are redefining what

9. See http://haywoodstreet.org.

missional community looks like in rural contexts. Together with the faculty the students spent a lot of time on cultural exegesis, learning about the many subcultures of Asheville and the surrounding areas. We went contra dancing at Warren Wilson College, floated the French Broad River, enjoyed the weekly drum circle in downtown Asheville, hiked the Blue Ridge Mountains, and worked in church-sponsored community gardens. We participated in the dedication of two new monastic houses, and worshiped in a rural hillside church in a heartbreakingly beautiful worship service called New Harmony that combines Taize chant with Appalachian folk hymns, icons, and candles.

After a few weeks of this new way of experiencing theological education with the faculty, one student said she would never be able to go back to a non-contextualized theology class. Her appetite for sterile classrooms had been ruined. My colleague who taught a doctrine class in his theological tradition said that teaching it in an ecumenical setting caused him to think in new ways about his own doctrine, because he could not assume that everyone was already committed to his theological tradition. For myself, teaching the evangelism class was sheer joy. Every day that our class gathered for prayer, learning, meals, ministry, fun, and at times, for struggle, I knew that all of us were being shaped and formed in powerful ways that would yield missional fruit for years to come.

At the time of this writing I am working with several organizations and institutions, including some of the most prestigious seminaries in the United States, to make the Summer Immersion an ongoing program. It is my dream to see our mainline seminaries model the kind of collaborative, creative, risk-taking leadership across institutional lines that church leaders of the future need to embrace.

A New Day for Theological Education

As we move into the future we are going to need more experiments with new models of theological education that equip ordinary Christians for significant missional work. We can no longer count on a professionalized ministry model to take the church in the direction the Spirit is calling. Theological education must become accessible, affordable, and adaptable. It must become kenotic.

Recently at a symposium on the future of theological education sponsored by the Association of Theological Schools, Executive Director Daniel Aleshire described the evolution of theological education over the past 200 years.[10] In the decades preceding the Civil War, he said, preparation for ministry meant shaping the minister so that he (and it was "he") would be an erudite, intellectual leader of the political community as well as a spiritual shepherd within the church. Theological education was shaped to create that kind of learning outcome.

After the Civil War, however, for a variety of social, economic and political reasons, the focus shifted so that the primary goal of theological education became the preparation of a modern minister who was professional and effective, who could lead the church toward success. Of course, success was measurable numerically by church membership and giving. This model of theological education dominated the mainline scene until the late twentieth century. This model is now in steep decline, with seminary enrollment in traditional masters of divinity programs shrinking in direct proportion to the general decline of the church.

The forms of theological education now emerging that will become the most prevalent forms in the next decades, said Aleshire, are those that focus not primarily on intellectual rigor, as if to prepare people to teach in a university, and not on businesslike efficiency and success as if the church were a business, but upon "soul formation." Cultivating persons in deep practices of prayer and theological reflection that lead to shalom inwardly, outwardly, and communally will not replace the importance of intellectual virtue or the necessity for fruitful work habits. But the priority must shift to matters of holiness and wholeness. This must become the central principle in our preparation of women and men for Christian leadership.

10. Aleshire, "2021: A Theological Odyssey."

The other trend that we are seeing in theological education is a need for shorter programs that equip laity or bi-vocational pastors for non-traditional ministries, especially in the non-profit world, in social change, in poverty alleviation, in interfaith spiritual community formation, and the like. Many schools are undergoing radical curriculum review to try to find ways to accommodate the needed change, but institutional wheels of change turn slowly, indeed, especially in university-based seminaries. Part of the slowness to change is an accreditation system based around and dependent upon models of theological education that no longer work. Innovation is very difficult for schools if doing so brings the threat of losing the Association of Theological Schools imprimatur.

In short, the sharp lines of division between academy, church, and mission no longer make sense in our cultural and ecclesial contexts. We must create seminaries for the laity that mobilize the laity for mission, seminaries grounded in local and regional churches, seminaries that combine the contemplative orientation of a Benedictine monastery with the activism and community organizing foci of the historic black church. Theological education for a new day must learn how to conduct hybrid learning using the very best technology available, coupled with on the ground mentoring, shared ministry, spiritual direction, and community life.

The day of bitterly competitive politics between theological seminaries in the same denomination must give way to a new day of collaboration and creative sharing of resources. The day of professionalized ministry among a permanently immature and sterile flock must yield to a new day when, in the words of Abbot Jerry Moore, "every Christian puts on his or her baptism" and welcomes a missional life.

For Reflection:

1. *What would you love to see included in new forms of theological education for the church?*

2. How can the church help seminaries and schools of theology make the necessary shifts in curricula and ethos?

3. How can the church and seminaries create strong equipping programs that are accessible, affordable, and adaptable?

PART TWO

A Field Guide to Starting Missional and New Monastic Communities in Historically Mainline Traditions

6

The Gift of Failure

In this chapter we consider the vital role of failure and mistakes in the process of community formation as well as life. We think about the pervasive shame in our culture that feeds perfectionism and makes it hard to take risks, and some of the elements of healing from that shame.

HELPING PEOPLE TO FAIL boldly is one of the greatest tasks in pioneering new forms of ministry. Without this essential life skill none of us would have learned to ride a bicycle, read, play a musical instrument, cook, play sports, or experience intimacy! Yet in the church it is often very difficult for someone who tries something new and fails to simply learn from the error and become more skilled. Rare is the Christian community that encourages its members to risk boldly, fail gloriously, learn, and grow without shame. Most of us have been in situations in the church where we proposed an idea for something and a curmudgeon said, "We tried that once and it didn't work. We'll never try anything like that again!" This attitude is based in fear and shame and it suffocates the creative energy of the congregation.

Toxic shame is one of the most powerful, debilitating emotions we can experience. It is different from healthy shame, which helps us realize we made a mistake and need to do something about it. (I.e., healthy shame says, "I am so dismayed and sorry because I forgot to pick up my ten-year-old son after school and he sat there for an hour before I remembered. Next time I will make sure to set my alarm on my phone.")

Toxic shame is the underlying conviction that "I am a mistake. I am inherently defective and deficient." Toxic shame is a combination of embarrassment and grief, and includes a sense of alienation and a need to hide either literally or in some symbolic way. One of the most common and pervasive aftereffects of abuse, especially sexual abuse, is toxic shame. Toxic shame both drives and is the result of many addictions. The elective cosmetic surgery industry as well as the advertising industry intentionally tap into our unhealthy shame in order to sell products. (I.e., "My nose/hair/hips/car/jeans are defective. . .if I have a nose job/hair implants/liposuction/a Lexus/Abercrombie and Fitch I will be lovable and worthy. I will be happy and my life will have meaning.")

Many of us grew up in shame-based families, including alcoholic families, drug addicted families, toxically religious families, and workaholic families. Some of us bear unjust cultural shame because of our ethnic or racial heritage in an Anglo-dominated culture, or because we are gay in a homophobic culture. While it is beyond the scope of this chapter to discuss in detail the causes of toxic shame, its manifestations, and what it takes to heal, suffice to say that it is one of the most debilitating psychological forces with which most of us must contend on our way to shalom.[1] Often people who are bound by shame find that their greatest fear is fear of failure. The healing of shame opens us to the process of failure as a normal part of human life, and something that can help us to learn and grow and that can form us into compassionate people.

---

1. For good book and video resources on healing from shame we recommend John Bradshaw's work, which may be found at this website: http://www.johnbradshaw.com/healingtheshamethatbindsyou1hourlecture.aspx.

If we can help each other view failure and error as useful teachers, we will not only be more humble, gracious, and compassionate when we ourselves fail, but we will be able to help one another gain wisdom and not take ourselves too seriously. So, expectations of failures large and small as well as success should be communicated during information sharing about *the pilot*.

Failure and the Pilot

It is best to approach the first year of forming a missional community as a pilot project so that everyone involved knows that it is an experiment that will involve trying things and then evaluating them. With pilots, people on the team and the anchor congregation(s) expect your team to learn by trial and error, and when everyone knows it is a pilot they do not go into the adventure expecting to quit in shame if a mistake is made. As you describe to your congregation and potential participants the role of a pilot as a testing ground or a laboratory where we learn through trial and error, you can begin to build into the culture of the future micro-community an appreciation for risk, experimentation, and the growth-producing role of failure. It is far easier to form this "low control/high accountability"[2] risk-taking DNA in a new community than to introduce it into an established community.

The most hoped for outcome of the pilot community, of course will be the formation of a sustainable missional community led by a team of several people. Yet even if at the end of the pilot the group decides not to continue, the experience of having followed a common rule of life with covenant accountability will bring gifts and impact that will last long after the pilot is over. This journey is worth the effort no matter what the outcome is.

Having said all of that, it is good to know that some mistakes and headaches can be avoided with good planning. For example, starting with an already developed and proven rule of life will help

---

2. Breen and Absalom describe the low control/high accountability dynamic as an essential element of the missional community, in their book, *Launching Missional Communities*.

you move forward more fruitfully than spending months trying to design a unique rule of life. Your team can always modify or replace the rule of life you start with after you've used it for a year.

Training the whole team in the new paradigms is another way to head off many problems before they begin. So is educating the anchor church if your community is going to be anchored in an established congregation. Those are topics of an upcoming chapter, so we will not go into detail about that here.

In closing, let us remember that even St. Paul and his lead team learned through trial and error as they pioneered their missional work.

> Paul and his companions traveled throughout the regions of Phrygia and Galatia because the Holy Spirit kept them from speaking the word in the province of Asia. When they approached the province of Mysia, they tried to enter the province of Bithynia, but the Spirit of Jesus wouldn't let them. Passing by Mysia, they went down to Troas instead. A vision of a man from Macedonia came to Paul during the night. He stood urging Paul, "Come over to Macedonia and help us!" Immediately after he saw the vision, we prepared to leave for the province of Macedonia, concluding that God had called us to proclaim the good news to them. (Acts 16:6–10, CEB)

Like the Apostle Paul, may we follow the Holy Spirit, going through doors that open, giving thanks when doors close, learning from our failures, and finding ways to be good news no matter what!

For Reflection:

1. *Sit quietly for a few minutes and think back to how your family of origin framed failure when it happened in the family. What were some specific events of failure? How did your parents or other caregivers respond? How did you respond? What was the emotional climate of your home when a family member failed?*

2. *Now ask the Holy Spirit to help you remember a time in your adult life in which you experienced failure. Ask for insight into some of the gifts that have come to you through that failure.*

3. *Finally, journal with this prompt: "When I think about starting a missional community and having it fail, I imagine . . ."*

4. *In prayer, offer to the Trinity what you have journaled about imagined failure. Imagine wrapping it in a gift box and handing it to the three. Then watch to see what happens next. Journal your experience of this meditative prayer.*

7

Disciple Formation in Missional Communities

In this chapter we will consider a holistic process of disciple formation that is oriented much more toward practice than toward subscribing to a set of theological ideas. The ideas matter, but have to be grounded in real practice. We will think about this for persons of all ages. The premise in this chapter is that rule-of-life communities are inherently more effective in forming deep discipleship than any other method.

Discipleship as a Three-Legged Stool

Often I (Elaine) am asked a set of questions that go something like this: "But how do you form disciples in missional communities? How do you make sure that people learn correct doctrine and do not deviate into some kind of heresy? How do you prevent a cult from forming? And what about children? How do you provide Christian education for them? Isn't this whole missional, new monastic thing for young adults who don't have families?"

It is hard not to chuckle, but I try. These are questions that understandably emerge from a vision of church that has been shaped by a professionally led, program driven ecclesiology and a building centered concept of the church. The questioners imagine that discipleship formation is mostly about learning to adhere to correct doctrinal formulations and not allowing dangerous theological diversity. They usually think of cult formation being a great danger in missional communities because the church cannot control the conversations and activities that happen off campus, away from the church building. There is also the fact that cults *have* formed from splinter groups in the past, but more about that in a moment.

The idea that children might more effectively learn what it means to believe and follow Jesus by actually believing and following Jesus in mission with a multi-generational community, than they will in a classroom with Sunday school curriculum and a video, well, that boggles the mind.

Let's imagine disciple formation as a three-legged stool. The flat part of the stool you sit on is doctrine. The three legs that support the seat are sets of practices. One leg is a set of practices called prayer. Another leg is a set of practices called hospitality. The third leg is a set of practices called justice.[1] The entire stool is able to support the weight of human life individually and corporately when all the pieces are in place. Disciple formation requires formation in all the practices as well as beliefs. But practices are foundational. This is why in the early church Christianity was simply known as "the Way."

Diana Butler Bass in *Christianity after Religion* reminds us that the old English word "believe" in Middle English really meant "be-love," or something like "love and trust." She asks a wonderful question: What would it look like if when we recited the Nicene Creed instead of saying "We believe in one God, the Father Almighty . . ." we said, "We love and trust in one God, the Father Almighty?"[2]

---

1. I realize that the word *justice* has been hijacked for political reasons, thus has become repugnant to persons who consider it a "liberal" word. But this is an old fashioned Bible word, found plentifully in the Bible, including Micah 6:8 (CEB): "He has told you, human one, what is good and what the Lord requires from you: to do justice, embrace faithful love, and walk humbly with your God."

2. Bass, *Christianity after Religion*, 128–34.

Bass is convinced that to form disciples who truly follow Jesus, we must first invite people to belong, to participate with us in our community. In the process of belonging and journeying with us in our community life, friends learn by watching and practicing with us, how to live a Christian life, how to be people of prayer, hospitality, and justice. Beliefs—the articulation of what we love and trust about God and the mission of God in the world—emerge from belonging and behaving.[3] As we belong and behave we grow in our ability to "be-love," to love and trust God.

Rule of Life

This is where a rule of life can be a huge help. A good rule of life such as the Rule of St. Benedict or the one used by the various Missional Wisdom communities[4] is a supportive structure that helps us learn the essential practices together with their theological foundations. Rule of life community helps us remember to be attentive to many ways of praying, the theology and practice of hospitality on many levels, and the theology and practice of justice in many contexts. By following a rule of life together, and having covenant accountability in small groups for how we are following it, we have ongoing opportunities to build a strong, solid three-legged stool of discipleship.

The use of a covenant group for disciple formation is basic to Wesleyan spirituality as well as most other Christian traditions, at least early in their history. Eighteenth-century Methodists called these groups "classes and bands." This kind of group was the backbone of the seventeenth-century German Lutheran Pietist movement promoted by Phillip Jacob Spener in his manifesto, *Pia Desideria*.[5] Scottish and English religious dissenters of the sixteenth and seventeenth centuries also had such groups, called

---

3. See ibid.

4. Such as New Day, the Epworth Project, and the Academy. See www.missionalwisdom.com.

5 *Pia Desideria* means "pious desires." An online edition of this spiritual classic can be found at http://www.ctlibrary.com/ch/1986/issue10/1029.html.

"conventicles," which were the cause of much persecution. In Latin American Catholic contexts similar groups became common in the mid-twentieth century and were called Base Communities and were shaped by liberation theology.[6] The list goes on. The idea behind all of these communities is that ordinary Christians are meant to live a radical life of discipleship that involves not just what we believe intellectually, but how we practice prayer, hospitality, and justice. Every reform movement in the history of the church has had some element of accountable discipleship for ordinary Christians, meeting in small groups.

Below is the Rule of Life followed by the lead teams of the People of New Day, along with the covenant questions that are used twice a month in covenant groups. When people consider their own pilots of new monastic communities, I recommend that they use the New Day Rule of Life for the first three to six months. It is easier to start with a good template and practice it from the beginning, so as to instill the DNA of being a rule of life community, than to try to add it later after people have established a habit of a community without a rule. Having the rule, using it, and being accountable is one of the surest ways to move deeper into genuine discipleship.

The New Day Rule of Life and Covenant Group Questions[7]

Rule of Life

Prayers

- We will pray daily

---

6. For more on Base Communities see http://en.wikipedia.org/wiki/Christian_base_communities.

7. The New Day Rule of Life and Covenant Questions may be found online at www.missionalwisdom.com/new-day/rule-of-life.

- We will use a variety of forms of prayer such as the reflective reading of Scripture and other spiritual texts, confession, the prayer of examen, intercession, journaling, and contemplation
- We will fast from food once a week (either a full or partial fast)

Presence

- We will practice a contemplative stance in order to be present to God, the world, and ourselves
- We will be hospitable to our neighbors in our families, neighborhoods and workplaces
- We will be hospitable to our faith community through participation in our worship, fellowship and mission

Gifts

- We will honor and care for the gift of the earth and its resources, practicing ecologically responsible living, striving for simplicity rather than excessive consumption
- We will practice generosity in sharing our material resources, including money, within and beyond this community
- We will use our spiritual gifts, talents and abilities to serve God within and beyond this community

Service

- We will serve God and neighbor out of gratitude for the love of God
- We will practice mutual accountability with a covenant group within the community, for how we serve God and neighbor

- We will practice regular Sabbath as a means of renewal so that we can lovingly serve God and neighbor

Witness

We will practice racial and gender reconciliation
- We will resist evil and injustice
- We will pursue peace with justice
- We will share the redeeming, healing, creative love of God in word, deed and presence as an invitation to others to experience the transforming love of God

I commit to this rule of life and to the well-being of this community, out of gratitude to God who forgives, heals, and makes all things new. May my life be a blessing within and beyond God's church, for the transformation of the world.

Covenant Questions

Prayers

How did you experience prayer since we last met?
- How did you experience fasting since we last met?
- How can we support you in the development of your prayer practices?

Presence

In what ways were you present to your inner life? Your significant others? Your work or school associates? Your neighbors?
- How did you practice hospitality to your neighbors in your family, neighborhood, and workplace since we last met?

- How have you been present to our faith community through participation in our worship, fellowship and mission since we last met?

Gifts

Since we last met how have you honored and cared for the gift of the earth and its resources? How have you practiced ecologically responsible living, striving for simplicity rather than excessive consumption?

- In what ways have you practiced generosity in sharing your material resources, including money, within and beyond this community since we last met?

- How have you used your spiritual gifts, talents and abilities to serve God within and beyond this community since we last met?

Service

As you served God and neighbor since we last met, how have you nurtured a spirit of gratitude within yourself?

- In what ways have you struggled with temptation and sin since we last met?

- How have you practiced Sabbath for your own rest and renewal since we last met?

- How can we support you in your journey toward wholeness and trust in God's love until we meet again?

Witness

In what ways have you been an active agent of reconciliation since we last met? How can we support you in this process?

- In what ways have you engaged in resistance against evil and injustice since we last met? How can we support you in this process?

- In what ways have you shared the redeeming, healing, creative love of God in word, deed, and presence as an invitation to others to experience the transforming love of God, since we last met?

Leaders and Lead Teams

One of the best ways to prevent a cult from forming, and to keep weird theology from taking the missional community in unhealthy directions, is to practice shared leadership with a team of five to seven people, in which the lead team follows and is accountable for a healthy rule of life. Cults are always led by charismatic, controlling, and narcissistic individuals who do not like to share power or be challenged. Those kinds of leaders are deeply resistant to the kind of missional communities and new monastic communities this book is about. Instead of helping others become disciples of Jesus, cult leaders focus on developing "disciples" who blindly follow themselves into bondage and often, tragedy. Jim Jones and David Koresh are examples of this kind of cult leader.[8] Cult leaders also isolate their followers from family and friends, the opposite of the kind of networking and collaboration that mark healthy missional community.

Shared leadership for a missional community opens the path for an ongoing process of mentoring new leaders who learn to follow the rule of life, who learn to share leadership tasks and accountability with the other team members, and who learn to multiply communities by multiplying teams of leaders. When everyone

8. For the story of Jim Jones (who started out as a Methodist pastor!), and the People's Temple which ended in mass suicide in 1978, see http://en.wikipedia.org/wiki/Jim_Jones. A more recent tragedy involved David Koresh and the Branch Davidians, a cult whose compound was destroyed by the FBI in a siege near Waco, Texas, in 1993. See http://en.wikipedia.org/wiki/David_Koresh.

on the lead team learns how to prepare a worship gathering with another person, including being ready to guide the communal sermon, planning music, prayer, and other liturgical acts, a great deal of learning takes place around doctrine and practice. The actual act of leading worship further develops leadership skills and the ability to share one's faith, which are also part of discipleship training. The sharing of caregiving of community members results in a whole team of people who are comfortable praying for others, who know how to make hospital calls, and who become skilled at knowing when and how to refer folks for counseling. This organic multiplication and sharing of leadership on an ongoing basis is the way new lead teams are grown so that new communities can be launched and more disciples can be cultivated.

Just a few last comments are in order as to how missional communities of the sort that I am describing actually prevent cultishness or heresy. Having several voices and not just one guiding the theological conversation helps to prevent rather than cause theological dysfunction. And of course, remaining connected to the larger church rather than becoming isolated is another way to prevent cultishness in missional communities. This is one of the reasons Jonathan Wilson-Hartgrove recommends that new monastic communities remain attached to the institutional church.[9] And it is one of the reasons that in the Missional Wisdom Foundation we recommend that communities like New Day be anchored in an established church when possible.

Last but not least . . . a very good case could be made that a consumer model of church is heretical because it is based on personal preferences, tastes, and comfort rather than the mission of God.

For Reflection:

1. *How might children's spiritual formation be enhanced rather than diminished if they are fully included in a worshiping*

---

9. This is the theme of Wilson-Hartgrove's book, *New Monasticism*.

missional community? Think creatively about the various shapes such formation might take. What would be fun about it? What would be taxing? How could the whole community share responsibility for the children's theological education?

2. Even though most of us haven't thought of it this way, we all live by a set of habits that could be framed as our rule of life. What are some habitual practices you already have that lead to deeper shalom for yourself, your family, and neighbors? What are some habitual practices you would like to give up? Take up?

3. When you think about gathering a team of friends to follow the rule of life with you, what is the biggest challenge? How might you begin the conversation? Are there already some individuals whom you think would be interested in being in the pilot with you, following the rule of life with covenant accountability?

4. If you wish, create a work of art (a prayer, poem, painting, sculpture, song, or dance) that reflects your dream for developing a lead team that follows common practices of prayer, hospitality, and justice.

8

Gathering a Lead Team
for a Missional Community

In this chapter we will consider who might be good candidates to invite on to a lead team for a missional community, who needs to be invited even if they never participate, and how to begin gathering and forming the team during the pilot year. In this chapter, "missional community" refers to a gathered group of people who do not necessarily live in the same house but who are a worshiping and serving community. Other chapters focus on gathering people for residential intentional community. "Anchored" refers to an off-campus missional community that is connected to an established congregation.

For some who are reading this book, the matter of finding others to go on the missional journey with you is not an issue. You and a group of friends have already been talking about doing something like this for a while, and you are ready to take the next steps of organizing. But for others a lead team must be gathered. One of the first tasks is to look around your circle of friends and acquaintances, both inside *and outside* the church. It is likely that there are great candidates right under your nose.

76

To get started with noticing who might be a good fit, look for:

a. Someone who has expressed a desire to go deeper into discipleship, who wishes he or she could be in partnership with a small number of people for a shared journey of faith formation. This may be someone new to the church or it may be someone who is tired of serving on committees is and looking for "something more."

b. Someone who has said they understand that missions trips to other places of the world matter, but that we really need to be more involved in our own backyard because there are plenty of hurting people right here at home. This may be the person who volunteers in various humanitarian initiatives outside of church, and is more informed than most people about issues of justice. Or it may be a quiet soul who doesn't speak up a lot most of the time, but has a compassionate heart. Don't overlook retirees.

c. Someone who is always eager to sign up when you do have a short-term mission trip or some kind of local mission engagement because they like to be hands-on and make a difference in the world. This person may be someone who never reads the Bible and doesn't like "touchy feely groups," or someone who sleeps during sermons. But he or she is the first one to sign up to help others with disaster relief.

d. Someone who is a great listener, who can be with people as they are and not impose an agenda on relationships with others. This may be the older woman who doesn't think of herself as especially gifted, but perfect strangers routinely approach her in the produce aisle of Safeway, to pour out their hearts because she seems like a safe person to talk to. Or it could be someone who has had training in Stephen Ministries but would like to be more engaged in caring ministry with people outside the congregation.

e. Someone who is compassionate, open to new people and new experiences and is inherently hospitable toward others even when the others are *very* different from themselves. This person may be the one who at Thanksgiving and Christmas doesn't have many biological family members around the table but whose house is filled with a motley crew of people from diverse backgrounds, including homeless folks and stranded college students. She or he may be the person who participates in the AIDS walk and makes sure the church knows about human trafficking, PTSD among wounded veterans, environmental threats, and other challenging justice issues.

f. Someone who is not already weighed down with responsibility for time intensive ministries within the church (such as the administrative board chair, the warden, the choir director, the children's pastor, or the chair of the staff parish relations committee), since forming a missional community needs to be the primary ministry task of the persons on the lead team. The exception would be someone who has had heavy leadership responsibilities in the church but now wants to take a sabbatical from her or his usual roles in order to devote energy to the pilot.

g. Someone who is relatively new to the church, who is interested in doing something in ministry but hasn't felt drawn to the programs inside the church. This person may have interesting talents that don't fit with existing foci in the church, such as bartending, beekeeping, clogging, rock climbing, or gardening, the kind of skills that could be perfect for gathering a community around a common adventure. (We can hear some of you snicker about gathering a community around bartending, but pub churches are one of the fast-growing expressions of missional community!)

h. Someone who is on the margins of mainstream church culture but is still in your circle of contacts—high school students who don't like typical youth group activity; college students who don't come very often because they are tired, and church is on Sunday morning, or seems irrelevant; or young adults who grew up in the church but left after high school because it doesn't seem to connect with their lives. This person may be clean cut and have a type A personality, or they may be into death metal and piercings, or anything in between.

i. Someone who just doesn't fit well in typical church activity but who is spiritually hungry and seems to be open and seeking a more meaningful spiritual community. He may be a redneck who loves his deer stand or she may be into yoga. Perhaps this person is part of the LGBT community and has not felt welcome in church despite his or her deep spirituality and wisdom. Perhaps he or she is married to someone from another religion and previous church experiences with their partner have felt awkward.

j. "People of Peace" (a term from Luke 10:5–6) who are not part of any church but are in the neighborhood or community where you are interested in forming a missional micro-community, and they are hospitable to you. They welcome you into friendship and into their circles of friends, culture, and activities. Mike Breen and Alex Absalom have a fine section about finding "people of peace" in their book, *Launching Missional Communities.*[1]

Invite any and all of these persons especially to participate in a six-week study of *Longing for Spring* (especially geared toward various Wesleyan traditions), or of the first half of *Missional.Monastic.Mainline.* (geared toward historic mainline traditions), both of which offer an accessible introduction to missional and new monastic communities and the long history of missional micro-communities over the past 2000 years. These two books also have study guides to be used with a weekly small group experience.

This six-week study will provide an opportunity to cast a vision about missional communities, identify persons who may be called to be part of the pilot group that will in the fullness of time birth a lead team, and begin a discernment process that is transparent to the entire congregation for those groups that plan to be anchored in an established church. The twelve-month pilot

---

1. Breen and Absalom, *Launching Missional Communities.*

community begins after the six-week study is finished, with the people who want to continue and be part of the pilot. At the end of the twelve-month pilot those who discern a call to be on the lead team will become the team that leads the new missional community. When the newly born community begins meeting weekly for worship and fellowship, it will already have critical mass as a community because of the lead team. It will already have some grounding in the neighborhood and a good set of discernment skills in the making. It can turn its attention directly to missional engagement.

Throughout the preliminary vision casting, the six-week study, and the twelve-month pilot experience, it is important to be transparent with the anchor congregation (if there is one) about the process. Provide enough information about what is happening so that persons in the congregation feel included even if they don't want to participate in the new work. This is especially true of congregational leaders, such as board chairs, who don't have time to take on anything else because their plates are already too full. They still need to know what is happening because it is their job to take care of the institution of the local church. As Alan Roxburgh and Scott Boren note in *Introducing the Missional Church*, you will need the board's good will and need to report back regularly on missional experiments if the missional community is going to be anchored.[2] The bottom line is, people who love serving on boards, vestries, presbyteries, and the like in the church are usually not the ones who are interested in pioneering new forms of ministry, even when they are glad to support those endeavors by others. The skill sets required for spiritual entrepreneurship and for maintaining institutions are both important but very, very different.

Clergy and Influencers

Be sure to invite the clergy, staff, and every single influencer in your congregation to come to the six-week study, if your missional

2. Roxburgh and Boren, *Introducing the Missional Church*, 171–80.

community is going to be anchored. Let them know that you understand they may not be able to attend, but you want them to feel welcome and to know what is happening. This will help to prevent anxiety that you are starting a faction, a mutiny, a revolution, or heaven forbid, a cult.

An influencer is someone in the congregation who influences others' decisions and the general direction of the church. They may do this in healthy ways because others actively seek their wisdom and trust their judgment. Or the influencer may be dysfunctional and wield power through threats, shame, intimidation, and bullying. A church dominated by a dysfunctional influencer probably will not be a good candidate for an anchor church, and a bullying influencer will nearly always oppose the formation of missional communities because they threaten the bully's control. If you are a judicatory leader reading this book and wondering which congregations would be the best choice for anchor churches, think "healthy." Healthy means having a missional ecclesiology, a good relationship with its literal geographic neighbors and with other churches in the area, and a kingdom orientation instead of turf-mind. (Sadly, many congregations and clergy are more like street gangs than Christians when it comes to relations with other communities of faith.) The surest way to kill a missional community initiative is to try to use it to disinfect a toxic congregation.

Sometimes healthy influencers occupy key official lay leadership roles. Sometimes they do not. But within the group dynamics of the congregation an influencer can make or break anything new that is emerging, simply with his or her influence on the congregation. Many years ago I (Elaine) was appointed to pastor a small, declining congregation in the rust belt of northeast Ohio. During the years that I served there, one of the strongest influencers who helped to lead change was a woman in her late seventies who had a missional heart *and* the deep respect of the congregation. Nelle would come to administrative council meetings to help present the new ideas, and I can still hear her dear voice joyously saying to the council, "I'm just so *excited* about this new idea. It's going to help us reach those children/former members/college students/

inmates/shut-ins we've been missing!" It was very hard to resist Nelle's passion because she was a lifelong member who truly loved the people and they loved and trusted her. Nelle was the best kind of influencer.

Let the influencers know you value their perspective and presence in the congregation, and that you are hoping to introduce a new but very old form of disciple formation and missional outreach that draws from the best insight of your own tradition.[3] This means of course that you must become familiar with your tradition's history and theology, particularly the stories of the founding of your tradition and any reform and renewal movements in your tradition.

Without exception each of the mainline Protestant traditions were born out of renewal efforts that involved lay people meeting informally for spiritual formation, accountability, and missional engagement in the world. Use these stories to educate others. There is also a rich history of "old" monasticism in Catholic, Orthodox, and Anglican traditions from which we can learn.

For example in my tradition, Methodism, John Wesley was the founder whose vision was all about forming missional communities with a lay monastic ethos to renew Anglicanism, although he had his own language for the communities (classes, bands, and societies). While Wesley did not want Methodism to separate from the Church of England and become a competing denomination, eventually missional necessity (the need to ordain bishops who could ordain clergy to serve the sacraments) led to the birth of the Methodist Episcopal Church in North America. A generation after that birth Methodism in North America had begun to institutionalize and become complacent, so a reform movement—the Wesleyan holiness movement—broke out. The new movement had new wineskins: huge camp meetings for the teaching of holiness, and small groups called Tuesday Meetings for the Promotion

3. For example, as noted in chapter 7, Scottish Presbyterians have covenanters and conventicles in their story, and Roman Catholics have base communities. There are also wonderful stories of missional micro-communities in other Christian traditions outside of yours from which you may draw to inspire and cast vision with others.

of Holiness that evolved out of the old class and band meetings. (And you thought "missional community" was a mouthful!)

In teaching about missional community formation in Methodist or Wesleyan contexts I always refer to the stories, theology, and practices of both John Wesley, the father of Methodism, and Phoebe Palmer, the mother of the Methodist holiness movement, to ground the theology and practice of missional communities in Methodism. It is important for the influencers to know that what you are doing connects directly to their own tradition's best missional wisdom.

Let influencers know that you would welcome them to be part of the six-week reflection group that will lead to the formation of the pilot year. Explain that you are not expecting or requiring *them* to be in the pilot year, but you simply want them to be fully aware of the process the pilot group will undergo and learn more about how anchored communities relate to the congregation and the wider world. Help them understand that the six-week study will give good insight as to how anchored communities have the potential of helping the established congregation go much deeper in discipleship, as well as becoming a much more evangelistic and disciple-making church.

You simply must have at least one or two influencers who see the value of and bless and advocate for your endeavors, if you are going to be anchored in an established congregation. They will help in the future with support and interpretation among congregants as your missional micro-community begins to form and reach out. By attending to the inclusion of influencers you can prevent many unnecessary delays and conflicts and from the beginning you will have prayer, spiritual support, and encouragement from the anchor church.

Next Steps

The next step toward gathering a lead team is to invite everyone who has gone through the six-week study with you to prayerfully consider moving into a pilot year with you. While you will have explained to them from the first session in week one that this is going to be the next step after the six-week study, begin to ask them to pray about being in the pilot experience around week four of the six-week study, and repeat it for the next two weeks. In the sixth week ask for a commitment to pilot a year with you as a rule of life community. This means they will covenant with you to follow the rule of life and to meet weekly for spiritual formation, accountability toward the rule of life, and practices of discernment toward forming a missional community in which the pilot group would become the lead team. Explain to them that it will be best if they do not have many other ministry commitments in the church during the pilot year so that they can devote their ministry presence to the group experience.

Over the next twelve months of your pilot group use part of your time together for theological reflection that will build contemplative practices and cultivate accurate missional discernment and practice. Introduce them to books, web resources, people, and field trips that can open their hearts and minds to God's missional call. This can be accomplished by having a monthly focus for reading and reflection between times that your group meets, with some time spent each time you meet, sharing your reflections on what you have read. Make a plan for systematically imparting to your pilot group a missional imagination, a missional lens through which to read scripture, and missional ecclesiology.

A Typical Schedule for the Pilot Year

During the twelve months of the pilot group a weekly gathering can look something like this:

On the first and third weeks of each month:

6 p.m.: Gather for a simple dinner in one of the group member's homes. Hosting should take place on a rotating basis. The meal can be a potluck or be prepared by the host.

- 6:45—7:45 p.m.: Use the prayer of examen to discuss the common reading (or field trip, website, or other learning experience) that was assigned. That is, "What was most life-giving, and why? What was least life-giving, and why?"

- 7:45—8 p.m.: Close with prayer for one another regarding what surfaced as you reflected theologically and prayerfully about the common reading or other learning experience that was assigned.

On the second and fourth weeks of each month:

6 p.m.: Gather for a simple dinner in a member's home

- 6:45—7:45 p.m.: Covenant accountability for the rule of life. Take one of the five clusters of practices in the rule as the focus for the evening (rotating through the five systematically and repeatedly through the year). Each person should take a few minutes to share how they have experienced living with that part of the rule since your last check-in on the rule two weeks ago. The first time you have the covenant group, and from time to time thereafter, remind everyone of the need for confidentiality about personal sharing within the group, and be sure all the members are committed to it. A covenant document about following the rule together for a year and including the practice of confidentiality, that everyone signs at the beginning of the year, is a good idea.

- 7:45—8 p.m.: Pray for one another about whatever has surfaced during your time of sharing.

- 8 p.m.: Dismiss after reminding everyone of the next reading assignment or learning experience for the coming week.

For months with a fifth week, consider going on a field trip together, watching a movie that can inspire missional imagination, or some other activity that builds community and deepens your missional awareness.

For Reflection:

1. *As you consider various circles of friends and acquaintances, what are some circles or communities of which you are a part that are outside of the church? In what ways might people from that circle potentially be interested in a missional community gathered from or for that circle of people?*

2. *Who have been some of the influencers in your life? In your congregation(s)? How did they influence others?*

3. *Who is in your life now that might be a "person of peace," linking you to a community completely outside of the church?*

4. *When you think about starting a lead team and you imagine resistance from persons within the church, how do you feel? What are your thoughts? How do you imagine helping them to understand that a missional community anchored in your church would be true to your heritage and could be very helpful to the congregation?*

5. *The traditional Ignatian prayer of examen is a way of practicing discernment by noticing what is most life giving and most life draining in day to day life. (A good introduction to this practice is Matthew, Dennis, and Sheila Fabricant Linn's book,* Sleeping With Bread.) *As you think about the invitation to gather a group of friends for a six-week reflection group that births a pilot community that follows a rule of life together for twelve months, what do you find most lifegiving and most life draining about that prospect? What do you notice about yourself as you reflect on this question in God's presence? What is your petition to God in light of what you notice?*

9

Preparing the Congregation to Anchor
A Missional Community

In this chapter we will consider some of the best ways to help a congregation, especially its leaders, prepare to anchor a missional community. These preparations apply whether you are planning to launch residential or worshiping communities. Special preparations are needed if you are going to use church-owned property for your missional community, such as an empty parsonage.

AS I WRITE THIS chapter I (Elaine) am in the middle of companioning several churches, clergy, laity, and a district superintendent as they launch their first three missional communities in the Asheville area of western North Carolina. Yesterday a group of us descended on a spacious, newly updated brick parsonage in a mixed income neighborhood of Asheville. We were there to help the new house steward (leader of the new monastic community) move in. What a joyful time to see this dream become reality for many who have prayed, studied, and worked in preparation!

The house will be anchored in two churches. These are exciting days for everyone concerned! It requires time and diligent effort to prepare congregants and leaders to take this step of re-purposing an unused parsonage so that a new monastic community or missional worshipping community can be based there. These preparations are not complete even after the new community moves in, because throughout the first year or two of the missional community ministries there will need to be frequent dialogue between the people within the missional communities and the anchoring churches. Some questions and situations that will emerge cannot be anticipated. But much can be done to help a congregation prepare to anchor a missional community.

Sermon Series and Small Groups

In the year leading up to starting a missional community it is a good idea to develop a sermon series with coordinating small groups that takes the congregation through the Bible as the story of the missional God. Each sermon should draw from one of the major literary divisions of the Bible, such as creation stories, ancestral narratives, historical books, wisdom literature, prophets, Gospels, epistles, and Revelation. An eight-week series is ideal. These messages should always invite people into the adventure of life with the God who loves, heals, forgives, and makes all things new.

The small groups that could meet midweek, on Sunday evening, or during the Sunday school hour would have discussion questions and activities keyed to the major points made in the previous Sunday's sermon. To really maximize this coordinated learning effort, a daily devotional could be prepared for congregants to use Monday through Friday, so that when they arrive on Sunday at least some of them will have read and prayed with the text that is going to be used on Sunday. The devotional could be structured using the Order for Morning Prayer or something along those lines, so that the readings and journaling time are integrated into a daily office consistent with your tradition.

Follow this with a sermon series and coordinated small group plan (four to six weeks in length) that takes the congregation through their own denomination's history as a missional movement. This series should help members feel excited and proud of their own forefathers and mothers of faith. In my case the focus would be on Methodism's John Wesley and Phoebe Palmer, especially because of their seamless integration of a life of prayer and a life of justice. Every tradition has its own heroes of faith whom God called, to bring the gospel to the world. This series can help your congregation grow more rooted in its own tradition's missional theology, beyond the utility of the series in helping understand the purpose of the new, missional community.

The final sermon series and coordinated small groups could be short term as well, three to four weeks in length, focusing on the congregation's own missional context and the incredible gift of being able to participate with God in "good newsing" the world. Here is where you can especially highlight the way a church like yours can both attract people to the missional God, and can deploy people into mission with God through missional communities. Provide a clear outline of how your congregation's missional community is going to form with a pilot, a lead team, and so on. Let them know that the community will learn as it goes, celebrating successes and learning from mistakes.

Cultivate an attitude of joy and grace about this new ministry. You can coordinate these sermons, the small groups, and your initial lead team pilot group so that they are all happening at the same time for maximum impact, or you can work with the lead team first for a couple of months and then begin the sermon and small group series.

The reason I strongly encourage a sermon series *and* small groups is that people don't get to ask questions or share insights in a typical worship service, while they can do that in small groups. And by preaching through these themes you get to touch as many people as possible. If your sermons are podcast or in other ways distributed, even more people can hear the theology behind the new ministry. No one is left out of the vision-casting loop. A sermon series also helps the congregation feel confident that the pastor supports and is proud of their church becoming an anchor church.

A congregation whose pastor and leaders are ambivalent or opposed to the idea of missional communities will not succeed as an anchor. As soon as the missional community becomes fruitful, jealousy, anxiety, and everything from racism to a desire to exploit the communities financially will surface within the anchor church. The ambivalent pastor or lay leaders will almost always side with detractors in that case. A solid anchor church requires clergy and lay leaders with missional imagination, missional ecclesiology, wisdom, healthy boundaries, and a good sense of humor.

Sharing the Good News and Avoiding Burnout

From the very beginning of your year-long pilot group until the missional community is born, make the progress highly visible for the rest of the congregation. Always include the missional community on the prayer list for the church. Celebrate outreach events and other missional community happenings in the anchor church worship service with five-minute mission highlights, a monthly word from the team leader, and so on. Use video or PowerPoint slides to show pictures of what the missional community is up to. Pictures and video speak more powerfully than words. Keep the missional community and its work before the people so the whole church can feel proud of its missional community.

The start of any new ministry usually attracts that small handful of people who are already doing more than anyone else in the church. It will be important to explore with interested candidates their willingness to reduce commitments in other parts of their lives so that they have the time required to invest in the formation of the new community. Their pastors will need to be strong encouragers of this streamlining of commitments because often these good-hearted laypersons won't be comfortable disappointing the pastor.

When we started one of our New Day communities in Dallas, several busy church members joined in, thrilled to be part of the new endeavor. They were unwilling to let go of anything else they were already doing, however, and within a few months were feeling exhausted from attending worship and Sunday school on Sunday morning, New Day worship gatherings and community meals on Sunday evenings, lead team meetings twice a month on Monday evenings, several committee meetings per month for the anchor church, and so on, all of that on top of working fulltime and being responsible for their own families. These capable and loving people decided that after several months they simply could not continue with New Day without feeling like they had abandoned their previous commitments in the anchor church. They had to drop out.

Another potential obstacle is church leaders, including pastors, who fear the missional community will "cannibalize" the congregation by taking people away from the choir, committees, and Sunday school in order to populate the lead team of the missional community. In this case, especially if the pastor(s) are of this mind, the congregation is not yet a good candidate to be an anchor church. Anchor churches absolutely must have a healthy, missional ecclesiology. They must understand themselves as God's sent-out people. Otherwise they will sabotage the newly forming community with their insecurity and fear.

For missional communities *that are worshiping communities*, clergy and leaders in the anchor church need to clearly give lead team members permission *and encouragement* to step away from as many other anchor church responsibilities as possible, especially once the community launches with its missional outreach. Lead team members need to hear this message repeatedly: "You are our missionaries now in the _____ neighborhood. We are proud to designate that ministry as your ministry, and we do not expect or encourage you to devote your time to other activities in the anchor church. We do want to stay connected so that we can pray for you and support what you are doing. We do not want you to be overcommitted and not have time for your family, yourself, and rest."

Celebrate, Evaluate, and Innovate

At the end of the first twelve months, have a time to celebrate, evaluate, and innovate. Make this a festive event with food, video images of the year that has just gone by, stories, and liturgical acts.

A good way to evaluate is to ask these simple questions and simply discuss the feedback together:

What happened this year that we love?

What happened this year that was difficult?

What did we do that we want to continue?

What did we do that we want to change?

Where do we feel the Holy Spirit is leading us in the next few months? What are the signs that we are being led there?

How has the anchor church supported our missional efforts?

Are there additional ways the anchor church could support our efforts?

How have we kept connected to the anchor church?

Are there additional ways we might stay connected with our anchor church?

Give people a chance to step out of the pilot if they need to, without shame or judgment. Take time to renew the covenant for those who are going to continue into the second year after the pilot. Welcome new people onto the lead team as the Spirit leads.

What about the Money?

People will want to support the missional community financially, but in the U.S. at least, most people appreciate receiving a tax deduction for charitable contributions. For communities anchored in established churches, the church's non-profit status applies to the missional community, too. This detail in itself can make a big difference in the presence or absence of donations for missional outreach.

Another way that the anchor church can support the missional community is to be the financial administrator of offerings and expenses that come through the community. In this case the anchor church should create a line item in its budget for the community offerings once the community launches. Offerings should be taken to the anchor church treasurer and the lead team should be kept abreast of the fund levels and expenses through monthly reports.

This money should not be used for anything except the missional community. The lead team can determine, in group discernment, about expenses from the funds. This method keeps the administrative structure of the missional community more simple and transparent.

If the missional community has its own treasurer, a responsible system of accountability for funds received and spent should be implemented at the outset, for everyone's well being. Each denomination has guidelines for the establishment of a treasurer, financial secretary, and the handling of church funds. Those guidelines should be followed for missional communities, too, whether it is through the anchor church's financial system or within the missional community.

Insurance, Rent, and Church-Owned Property

As we were first starting our communities in Texas we found that there was anxiety in some anchor churches concerning liability and insurance. "Who will pay for the insurance?" trustees asked.

"Will the people living in the monastic house have Ministry Safe training?" pastors asked. "Will residents living in the parsonage-turned-monastic house pay rent?" asked some congregants. It is very important to develop a plan around these issues in order to provide a clear path for the community to both move forward in mission and in responsible stewardship of trust.

There will be many questions around finances, insurance, and liability that the anchor church and residential communities will need to consider. This is always the case for ministries happening off the main campus of the church.

Be certain to take the time to fully explain the details of the planned activities of the missional community to the people who handle the business aspects of the church. Expect them to have questions, and give them plenty of time to work through the details. It is very typical for the people who are working with the business aspects of the church to worry about the risks and costs of new and innovative ministries. Lawyers, bankers and accountants all earn their living by identifying and dealing with risks, and when they perceive themselves as being responsible for "safeguarding" the assets and ministries of the church, they are almost always inclined to say "no" to innovative ideas that involve meeting in places away from the church building, especially when those places have bedrooms.[1]

Expect that reaction and give those people the time they need to work through their initial concerns. Don't be surprised or hurt when the lawyers on the Administrative Board raise concerns—that is what they are trained to do—and don't see them as evil or unnecessarily conservative. Let them do what they do, and help them to overcome their concerns by giving them complete information, even about the things that you might be worried about. Home churches and new monastic communities are growing all

---

1. I often remind people who are opposed to doing any ministry in a house because of its perceived higher risk factor for sexual misconduct that in fact most clergy sexual misconduct and sexual abuse by ministry leaders happens in the pastor's office or in programs run by the church on the church campus.

over the world, and a little planning and preparation can go a long way in reducing the risks of operation to very manageable levels.

In most church insurance policies, all ministries of the church are already included in the policy, even if it happens off campus or at an extension campus. It is a simple matter to make clear with your insurance agent that your missional community is an official ministry of the anchor church. Usually this will not increase the cost of the policy, or only minimally. Early in the planning stages for a missional community, check the insurance policy and talk with your agent to find out about this.

For church properties that are being used for residential monastic communities, the church's liability insurance (slip and fall, etc.) is usually adequate for liability coverage. Residents in the monastic house should be responsible to purchase their own renter's insurance to cover their personal property in the case of theft, loss, or damage.

Every person in leadership in the church, whether their ministry takes place in a church building or off campus, should be trained with their denomination's version of Ministry Safe practices, to help support the right of all persons to be in a ministry setting where personal and sexual boundaries are respected.

In residential monastic communities some good policies to enact to maintain appropriate boundaries include:

1. Residents should each have their own rooms, and others are not to go into a resident's room.

2. Visitors who come for public times of prayer, community meal, or other public gatherings should know when the gathering ends and a clear signal should be given that it is time for persons not living in the house to leave. An easy way to do this after community meal and evening prayer, for example, is for the house steward to stand up and say, while walking toward the front door and opening it so that guests will leave, "We have loved having all of you with us this evening. We look forward to your return." Another good idea is to have public hours posted by the door so that people from the neighborhood know when it is okay to come for a visit.

3. Visitors who come for prayers, community meals and other public gatherings may only be in community gathering spaces, typically the living room, dining room and kitchen. A restroom should be designated for guests when possible so that residents' private space remains separate.

4. No sleepovers are allowed in residents' rooms unless the guest is a member of the resident's family.

A variety of approaches can work with regard to paying for the use of church owned property for missional communities. In a healthy situation the anchor church makes the property as accessible and inexpensive as possible for the missional community, because it is a ministry of the church. Often persons who choose to live in a new monastic community have already chosen downward mobility, a lower income, and a missional context for the sake of the gospel. The church should respect this deeply traditional commitment to simplicity and not make it harder for the residential community by charging an exorbitant rent or creating uncomfortable demands around property maintenance.

In one of our communities in Dallas, the Dietrich Bonhoeffer House, the Missional Wisdom Foundation entered into a contract with Grace United Methodist Church to use a church-owned house beside the church. The house was in poor repair and needed a good deal of renovation to make it habitable. After the MWF secured funds for renovation we leased the house for five years from the church for the cost of the renovations. The residents in the house, all of whom are students, pay their own utilities and maintain the yard using the church-owned lawnmower and rake. The students' rent is paid for by a scholarship. This arrangement has worked well since a third party (the MWF) is administering the community, but in the future it is possible that Grace UMC will not only anchor the Bonhoeffer House, but also administer the community. In that situation, residents could pay a very modest rent to Grace UMC to be used for upkeep of the roof, etc., or the church could simply write into its budget these items and continue to make the house available rent-free to carefully selected members.

Sometimes trustees or board members resist generosity in use of the unused parsonage as a monastic house, even if rent is assessed. In this situation the pastor(s) and perhaps other judicatory leaders will need to educate the resistant leaders about the house as an extension ministry of the church. If leaders continue to resist despite being informed, it may be wise to choose another church for an anchor, however desirable the unused parsonage may be. It is unfair to invite a monastic community to live and serve in a hostile or resentful anchor church.

One of the biggest assets of most historically mainline denominations is real estate that could be sold or repurposed for missional communities. Each denomination has its own policies around church real estate, but few of these policies have taken into account the possibility of missional communities. Judicatory leaders would be wise to spend time rethinking real estate, and work to free as much of the unused real estate as possible to either be sold and the proceeds invested in missional community formation, or repurposed for missional use.

Some closed churches, for example, are being transitioned into missional communities that include residential quarters (repurposed Sunday school wings), classrooms, community center space for neighbhorhood development, and the chapel for a daily office and retreat space.

Final Thoughts

One of the best gifts of healthy new monastic and missional communities is their ability to serve as a leavening agent in the anchor church. As persons living and serving in a missional community include members of the anchor church in community meals, prayer, and outreach in the neighborhood, the anchor church's understanding of discipleship deepens, and many others begin to live a more committed, vital spiritual life in their own homes and neighborhoods. A wonderful gift of the anchor church to the missional community is just that—an *anchor* of stability, love, prayer, and encouragement to its own missionaries.

For Reflection:

1. *What are your denomination's policies around unused buildings, parsonages, camps and retreat centers? Who would be the right conversation partners if a congregation wants to repurpose denominationally owned property for missional purposes?*

2. *For congregations that are used to using the lectionary for sermon planning, what are some creative and assuring ways that the congregation could be helped to suspend use of the lectionary during the weeks the sermon and teaching series on missional theology is introduced?*

3. *As you consider your own congregation, where is it right now in missional understanding? What kind of tending would it need in order to become a strong anchor church?*

10

Who, Where, Why, What, When

(Forming a Residential Community)

In this chapter we will consider some of the most important elements of forming a residential missional community, also called a new monastic community.

THE MOST DEMANDING EXPRESSION of missional community is a residential new monastic community guided by a rule of life. It is more challenging than a missional community that worships and serves together, because it involves the added dimension of living together. New monastic communities are based in a home that is focused on being a house of prayer, hospitality, and justice internally and externally. As we will see in a moment, there are several ways to configure a residential community, including non-related people sharing a house, an apartment complex, or living in the same neighborhood but with shared daily and weekly rhythms of prayer, hospitality, and service. This kind of ministry is popularly known as an "intentional community." Historically it is called monasticism.

Monasticism, New and Old

Shane Claiborne's book, *Irresistible Revolution: Living as an Ordinary Radical*,[1] chronicles the beginning of his community, Simple Way, in Philadelphia, and has sparked the imagination of thousands of young adults in the past several years who now live in intentional communities around the world. Wonderfully written, funny, and deeply prophetic, Claiborne's book indicts the contemporary church for having lost touch with its own theology especially in relationship to justice. Coming from an evangelical background, Claiborne calls the church to embrace the historic practices of monasticism that Methodists call "social holiness." He has special words of challenge to Methodists who have for the most part forsaken the original vision of John Wesley.

Shane's friend and one time classmate from Eastern University, Jonathan Wilson-Hartgrove, founded the Rutba Community in Durham, North Carolina and has become the leading writer in the new monastic movement. Wilson-Hartgrove along with his team launched the Schools for Conversion—weekend seminars that teach principles and practices of new monasticism. This initiative is now called Weekend Visits and takes place in many different new monastic communities.[2] One of Wilson-Hartgrove's most significant volumes on the development of communities is *New Monasticism: What it Has to Say to Today's Church*.[3] This

---

1. Claiborne, *Irresistible Revolution*.

2. See http://www.newmonasticism.org/weekend.php. The book that is used for instruction at Weekend Visits is Rutba House, eds., *School(s) for Conversion*.

3. Wilson-Hartgrove, *New Monasticism*.

book clearly defines the ways in which new monastic communities should remain rooted in the institutional church both for the renewal of the church and for the humility and accountability of the new monastic communities. A more recent publication, *The Awakening of Hope: Why We Practice a Common Faith,*[4] is a catechism that helps readers reflect upon core values that are common to intentional communities today.

Historically, monastic communities first arose after Christianity became the preferred religion of the Roman Empire, when Christians felt the church was missing the mark in its prophetic and priestly witness.[5] Communities formed in order to demonstrate a contrast society that more faithfully incarnated the life of Jesus. The early monastics such as St. Benedict of Nursia (480–543 AD), believed that small residential communities of Christians living by the gospel were the best expression of faith in a world that needed to know Jesus.[6] St. Benedict is considered the father of Western Christian monasticism because his rule of life set forth a path for communal living for lay Christians that was balanced and moderate, and that truly embodies the way of Jesus. The Rule of St. Benedict continues to be widely embraced around the world today, not only by Catholic Benedictine communities but also by Protestants who choose to be oblates,[7] and by some Protestant new monastic groups such as the St. Brigid of Kildare Methodist-Benedictine community founded by Mary Stamps.[8] Jonathan

4. Wilson-Hartgrove, *The Awakening of Hope.* This book also comes with a DVD that is helpful for group study.

5. See Heath and Kisker, *Longing for Spring,* 15–37, for a brief history of monastic reform movements.

6. For a short biography of St. Benedict of Nursia see http://en.wikipedia.org/wiki/Benedict_of_Nursia.

7. An oblate is someone who does not live in the residential community with others of the monastic order, but who follows the rule of life and participates with the residential community in a limited fashion.

8. Sister Mary Ewing Stamps, OSD, founded this community in St. Joseph, Minnesota in 1999. The community includes both women and men, and is both residential and dispersed (having persons who live in other places beyond the monastery).

Wilson-Hartgrove has written a wonderful little book about Benedictine spirituality for contemporary Protestant new monastic communities and others called *The Wisdom of Stability*, offering a scriptural analysis of the Benedictine Rule of Life.[9] Mary Stamps and Jonathan Wilson-Hartgrove's work is of special relevance to anyone from historic mainline traditions that is going to form a residential missional community.

Getting Started

Most intentional communities today begin in a rush of youthful idealism and quickly fail. Why? It is hard to live together. Just ask any married couple! Few of us learned good conflict resolution skills in our family of origin and all of us have issues of one kind or another. Even when everyone in the house is healthy, loving, and wise there is inevitable friction from time to time, and after the "honeymoon" wears off life in an intentional community can become as annoying and unfocused as life in any family. If the community practices a common purse the challenges can be even more rigorous. It is not easy to live together with integrity as disciples of Jesus committed to missional vocation in an individualistic and mobile culture. Intentional community is truly counter-cultural!

Yet it is possible to avoid many unnecessary headaches with some advance preparation and mindfulness. With sufficient external support, accountability, healthy boundaries, spiritual guidance, and a sense of humor, intentional communities can become potent gospel-bearers in a world hungry for God. We formed the Epworth Project in Dallas/Ft. Worth in order to help people who are called to this way of life be able to enter it with commitment and readiness.

The remainder of this chapter is intended to help you think about the major preliminary areas of preparation and formation that contribute to the founding of a healthy, vibrant intentional community. For a thorough, superb treatment of life together that

9. Wilson-Hartgrove, *The Wisdom of Stability*.

gleans wisdom from the study of many new monastic communities over the past several decades, see David Janzen, *The Intentional Community Handbook: For Idealists, Hypocrites, and Wannabe Disciples of Jesus.*[10] Having lived in an intentional community for the past forty years, Janzen knows from experience how challenging, yet how rewarding intentional community can be. Janzen's work guides readers through the processes necessary to establish a community from the first dream on into years of solidarity and fruitful ministry, including the multiplication of communities. It is an essential resource for any residential new monastic community.

Who, Where, Why, What, When: Discerning the Call

The most important question to address first is *who* will live in the new monastic community, not *where*. As always, the ministry is more about relationships than buildings! Often in American culture young, single adults are more interested in this way of life than are older people or those who are married and have children. This is partly because they have already experienced limited forms of communal life in college, the Peace Corps, or some other situation. Young adults are also more likely to create a surrogate "family" with a peer group instead of within their family of origin. So they are more likely to express interest in new monasticism than is, say, a fifty-year old-dentist with three kids in college.

However, the "new monasticism is a temporary fad for young adults until they get a real life" notion is actually a stereotype that should be dispelled at the outset. Intentional community can be a beautiful way to raise families or to create a loving residential environment for retirees. A great example of this is the ecumenical 18th Avenue Peace House in Portland, Oregon, led for more than thirty years by John and Pat Schwiebert.[11] An intentional

---

10. Janzen, *The Intentional Community Handbook*.

11. See http://18thavepeacehouse.org. This community was founded by John, an ordained elder in the UMC, his wife, Pat (a nurse), and several other couples who were committed to a simple, shared life (including a common purse) and rigorous peacemaking initiatives. They raised their families in the

community can provide a wonderful, supportive context for single mothers to raise their children, or for a multigenerational group of people to form an extended Christian family. It can welcome refugees, recovering addicts, persons with HIV/AIDS, and other persons in need of loving community during transitions in life.

Think about it. Throughout most of human history around the world people have lived with extended families and in villages or neighborhoods that are intentional communities. Contemporary "senior campuses" like the one where my (Elaine's) mother resides offer various configurations of housing and community life for retirees and are a common, secular expression of intentional community. There are of course Amish, Mennonite, and independent agricultural groups such as Homestead Heritage Farm[12] that live in intentional community. There is the Jewish tradition of the Kibbutz.[13]

Usually when I trace out the fear and negative stereotypes that questioners have about families living in community, it has more to do with 1960s hippie communes, open marriages and polygamy (!), and with American individualism than with the actual practice of communal life that has been the norm around the world for millennia. The rapidly growing secular Danish based co-housing movement offers abundant evidence for the preferability of living in community over isolation, when raising families.[14]

The best candidates for living in intentional community are persons who feel called into this way of life. It is helpful if the leaders or initiators of the intentional community are spiritually grounded and emotionally healthy. I specify "leaders and

rambling old home and today tend several members with Alzheimer's Disease and other disabilities. A house church called Metanoia Community also met in the Peace House for many years.

12. This industrious community is made up of a sizeable group of families who live simply, patterned after the Amish in many ways, but with a missional vocation to the world. See http://www.homesteadheritage.com.

13. See http://www.kibbutz.org.il/eng/.

14. To find out about the co-housing movement in the United States, see http://www.cohousing.org/what_is_cohousing.

initiators" in this way because a substantial number of wonderful intentional communities exist whose primary residents are persons with mental illness and various kinds of physical, spiritual, and emotional challenges. These communities were founded by leaders and initiators with a vision for the beauty an intentional community could provide persons with special needs. The L'Arche communities established by Jean Vanier and made famous by Henri Nouwen are a good example.[15]

The first set of discernment questions about *who* might be good candidates to live in community has to do with vision and call:

1. Have you had recurring thoughts and a dream to live in intentional community? In your dream, who lived with you?

2. Did you imagine living in your current location, expanding it to include others? Or did you relocate to a more suitable context?

3. Did you envision a specific ministry flowing out of your intentional community? If so, what was that like?

4. How can we in the church assist you in living into your call to intentional community?

I often meet pastors and lay persons who are excited about helping others form an intentional community as an extension ministry of their established church. Their interest comes from having read a book or heard a lecture about intentional community, combined with the fact that their church has an unused parsonage or at times a closed church building that could be rehabbed and used fruitfully for such ministry. In this case the house (or unused church building) is already available but the residents for the community have yet to be discovered. While it is much easier to begin with motivated people who want to live in community rather than beginning with an empty house, God is able to assemble an intentional community through many paths!

15. For more about L'Arche, see http://www.larcheusa.org/who-we-are/communities/.

In the case of the empty parsonage or other donated property some helpful lines of inquiry might include:

1. Is our unused parsonage/closed church building near a college or seminary campus? Do we have someone in our congregation who might love to steward (live with and lead) a residential community for college students, leading them in rhythms of prayer, hospitality, and missional engagement?

2. Is our potential house in a part of town where Americorps workers carry out their work? Could someone in our congregation steward (live with and lead) that house as a place for Americorps workers to live in intentional community?

3. Do we have some single mothers, widows, or others in our congregation who might be open to living together in intentional community in our church-owned property, carrying out a new ministry of prayer, hospitality, and missional service in the house and neighborhood? Does one of them already seem to show gifts for stewarding the house?

4. How can we collaborate with other churches within or beyond our denomination in our geographic area, inviting persons from other congregations to form an intentional community in our church-owned property? Is there someone in our circles who already shows signs of gifting for stewarding the house?

5. Is there a population we have been hoping to reach but have yet to connect with relationally around the church owned property, such as a Latino or Vietnamese neighborhood? Is there someone in our circles of ministry from that culture with the necessary language skills who might feel called to live there with a few other people in order to form the ministry there? Do our judicatory leaders have persons "in the pipeline" in seminary or elsewhere who might be perfect for this ministry? How can we find out?

6. Are there retired clergy who are already well established in a contemplative path who might gather and anchor a residential community in the church-owned property, devoted to contemplative ministries, spiritual direction, and retreat days in the house?

It is generally harder to start with a house and hunt for residents, than to start with people who are called and help them find the right place to live and serve. Yet the mainline church is now rich in unused real estate, including parsonages, church buildings, and camps and retreat centers, some of which would be ideal for intentional communities. With prayer, communication, vision casting, and persistence, I am convinced that any church that wants to anchor a new monastic community can find suitable persons to live and serve there.

The second set of discernment questions have to do with *where*. There are many options for places to develop intentional communities. Here, too, a sense of call is vital in determining the place where the community will be in mission. In the new monastic movement preference is given to locating communities "in abandoned places of empire," meaning the forgotten and neglected neighborhoods, both rural and urban, where a residential community can help bring about neighborhood transformation. Suburban contexts can also become locations for intentional community, as proven through the work of Hugh Halter and Matt Smay, whose Colorado suburban residential community is described in their book, *Tangible Kingdom*.[16] The key to the "where" is where the Holy Spirit is calling the community to form for missional reasons.

As mentioned previously, many churches now have unused parsonages that could become great locations for a residential community, especially in neighborhoods that are in transition. An empty parsonage can be leased at low cost or for utilities only to a new monastic community to enable engagement with the neighborhood and help the church connect with, love, and serve with neighbors that previously had been missed. This has been the case for the Dietrich Bonhoeffer House in Dallas, which is a ministry of

16. Halter and Smay, *Tangible Kingdom*.

Grace United Methodist Church in partnership with the Missional Wisdom Foundation. While Grace UMC has long been involved in numerous justice ministries especially with refugees, Bonhoeffer House has helped the church connect more deeply with persons without homes who live in the area. Bonhoeffer is also contributing to the formation of contemplative practices at Grace.

Is it better to have one house, several apartments, or something else? Intentional communities do not always require that members all live in one house together. A community can be formed by renting or buying several homes on the same block or in the same neighborhood or trailer park, with families and individuals meeting together several days per week for morning and/ or evening prayer, a weekly community meal, and regular outreach and engagement in the neighborhood. The key to success in this model is for members of the intentional community to leave plenty of space in the neighbhorhood for others rather than turning the entire neighborhood into a Christian fortress where outsiders are unwelcome. The idea behind new monasticism, after all, is that the new monks are missional, not cloistered.

The "why" of forming intentional community is an issue that should be revisited on a regular basis by persons living in community. It is easy to lose focus in the day to day struggles of mundane life and the clamor of many voices for our attention. When Dietrich Bonhoeffer coined the term "a new kind of monasticism" he said, "The Restoration of the church will surely come only from a new type of monasticism which has nothing in common with the old but a complete lack of compromise in a life lived in accordance with the Sermon on the Mount in the discipleship of Christ. I think it is time to gather people together to do this."[17]

Bonhoeffer, a German Lutheran pastor and resister of the Nazi regime, focused his doctoral dissertation on ecclesiology and the need for much deeper discipleship in the church. Among his other prophetic works, he formed an underground seminary to

---

17. This quote is found ubiquitously in new monastic circles but was originally penned in a letter from Dietrich Bonhoeffer to his brother, Karl-Friedrick, on January 14, 1935.

equip clergy who, like him, had chosen resistance. His book *Life Together* is essential reading for the church today, especially for persons called to live in intentional community. In Bonhoeffer's vision, the "why" is the living out of the Sermon on the Mount *as a community*.

The best way for a new monastic community to stay focused on the "why" is for it to follow a well thought-out rule of life together from the very beginning. The primary reason the Benedictines are still around and doing great ministry is that they are committed to living the Rule of St. Benedict! In our Epworth Project communities in Dallas/Ft. Worth, we use a rule of life based on United Methodist membership and baptismal vows. It is very similar to the New Day Rule of Life, but with some additional components having to do with sharing chores, handling conflict, and other homely aspects of daily life.

Remembering the "why" of the community is deeply connected to the "what." A new monastic community invites an ongoing experience of conversion that is brought about by living together in order to offer our neighbors a glimpse of heaven, a foretaste of the heavenly banquet.

One last component of the "why" that is important to mention and that can save much heartache is the application and review process. Every healthy new monastic community that I have visited or researched requires an application process of some kind, a probationary period, and a regular review process that helps with discerning who should live in the community and for how long. A good application process is a screening tool that assists people who are inside the house, as well as would-be residents, determine if applicants understand and are prepared to fully embrace the "why" of the community.

Early on in our formation of the Epworth Project we learned that we needed a good application and review process to prevent unfortunate situations in which persons simply wanted reduced rent or had some alternative agenda for the community that was counter to the community's DNA. Our application and covenant are now very clear and detailed, and are legal documents that protect everyone involved should the need arise to invite a resident to leave.[18] (Thankfully this is a rare occurrence.) At the Missional Wisdom website, you can find a sample application form for a residential community.[19] Feel free to adapt it for your use.

In the next chapter we will consider the vital role of an outside person or persons whose task is to provide spiritual and justice formation and pastoral care for those who live within the intentional community. The traditional name for this person is abbot or abbess. For now simply know that this ancient practice is vital to helping intentional communities reach their potential and remain right side up.

For Reflection:

1. *Have you ever visited intentional communities? If so, describe your experience. How did the people live? What was the history of the community? How did they structure life together, handle conflict, handle finances, raise children? What did you learn from them?*

   Imagine that you became part of an intentional community in your neighborhood. How would you explain it to your neighbors? How might an intentional community be a blessing in your neighborhood?

2. *What are the biggest challenges you would face in embracing a life of intentional community? What would be some steps you would take to address those challenges?*

   Imagine that your church had unused property that is well suited for a new monastic community. How would you cast the vision for this at your church? Who are people that you would want to invite to consider living there? Who would need to be

---

18. Our applications for various types of persons and communities are found on our website at http://missionalwisdom.com/epworth/applications/.

19. See http://missionalwisdom.com/epworth/applications/.

part of the conversation to help the dream move forward to reality?

3. Where are the intentional communities in your geographic area? What can you learn about their history, goals, leadership, and mission?

11

The Role of the Abbot

In this chapter we will reflect upon the need for someone who is outside of the residential community who can provide pastoral care, spiritual direction, and formative guidance in life together. Whether there is just one house or a network of them, whether or not the term "abbot" is used, this person is an invaluable part of the team.

THIS YEAR WE WELCOMED our first abbot, Reverend Jerry Moore, to the Epworth Project in Dallas/Ft. Worth. After five years of developing seven residential new monastic communities, we were ready for an abbot's presence and ministry. Up until Jerry joined our team Larry, Bret Wells, and I (Elaine) provided the guidance of abbots, but as our foundation grew this became more and more challenging. All of us have fulltime work that pulls us in many directions. We realized several months ago that it was time for us to make this shift. Our new abbot tends the monastic houses and is also developing retreat and spiritual direction ministries for area clergy who are feeling called toward emergence.

What is an Abbot?

The word *abbot* comes from the Semitic word *abba*, or father. In the ancient tradition of Christian monasticism the desert fathers (abbas) and mothers (ammas) guided persons who sought to live a more faithful, incarnational form of discipleship.[1] These individuals were typically older and wiser saints who had lived as Christians for a long time. They were deeply established in contemplative and ascetic practices. Years of prayer and reflection had taught them to "show up, pay attention, cooperate with God, and release the outcome." Though some of them were eccentric or tended toward extreme asceticism, in general their relationships with others were marked by compassion, wisdom, gentleness, courage, simplicity, and rhythms of life that alternated between solitude and community. They owned and used as few material resources as possible. The desert fathers and mothers were the early spiritual directors and pastoral counselors of the post-Constantinian church.

Today we need such persons to guide our new monastic communities. There are several reasons why this is so, but the biggest reason has to do with transitions. Very few middle class, upper middle class, or working class people who decide that it is time to form a residential intentional community are prepared for the transition to this way of life. Some of this has to do with natural life transitions, and some with the transition away from certain American cultural norms.

Why We Need Abbots for Intentional Communities

The majority of people who are drawn to intentional community today are young adults ages eighteen to thirty. These are the years when most of us are getting an education, figuring out who we are, attempting to individuate but stay connected to our families of

1. Throughout this book and elsewhere I use the term abbot to indicate either male or female leaders. Historically the term *abbess* was used for women, but as is the case with the word *actor,* now commonly referring to persons of any gender who are in the acting business, I see no need for gender distinction for titles of abbots.

origin, deciding where to work, whether we want to get married, and other decisions related to building the first half of life. Young adulthood is a time of profound transition out of childhood. Guidance from older, wiser, grounded people we trust is so much better than going it alone.

Yet older people do not find moving into residential community any easier than do young folk, because usually by mid-life we have a house full of stuff, we are set in our ways when it comes to habits of housecleaning, cooking, rhythms of work and rest, and the like. We are used to extreme privacy within the walls of our homes and are loathe to give up walking around in our underwear or simply having control of the TV. It takes a lot of adjusting to deconstruct the "necessity" of all that individualism and privilege. Having wise, perceptive companions is essential as we make the shift to community life in which our ego doesn't rule the roost.

These and other "stage of life" issues are challenge enough, but the most difficult obstacle for us has to do with our attitudes toward money and how those attitudes shape our relationships with our neighbors. American Christians have been deeply habituated to think of money as a sacred object, because our culture is one of market capitalism.[2] From infancy we are inundated with the constant message that happiness and well being come from buying and owning more stuff. We need more and more money to buy more and more stuff. The common wisdom is that you can never have too much money.

The more money and stuff we have, the more we worry about others with less money and stuff trying to take what is ours. So increased affluence tends to cause increased firewalls against other people who are "below" us economically. But affluence also creates barriers with others who are of equal net worth. In general the more affluent a neighborhood is, the less likely it is that neighbors know and spend time with each other. One of the few exceptions

2. For a wonderful little book about healing our attitudes toward money, see Dunn and Norton, *Happy Money*. Dunn and Norton offer a compelling argument that happiness comes not from spending money on stuff but on experiences. The happiest way of all to spend money is in using it to help other people be happy.

to this rule is the high-end retirement community where people purchase homes in order to be part of a village of like-minded, economically (and usually racially) homogeneous people.

We American Christians have uncritically imbibed these norms around money and relationships in ways that are mind-boggling in light of the teachings of Jesus. Materialistic values are evident in the opulence with which we build some church campuses and the expectations we have that senior pastors of premier tall steeple churches should live like corporate magnates. That materially affluent lifestyle includes being removed from the people you serve. I regularly hear seminary students describe churches according to how many doors you have to go through before you can get to the senior pastor. The more doors, the more prestigious the pastor is.

When newly elected Pope Francis eschewed the lavish papal quarters in favor of a simple apartment, the world was astounded.[3] They were even more shocked when at his first Holy Thursday service he washed the feet of inmates at a juvenile detention center.[4] Everyone expected him to go along with the opulent and distant norms.

Enculturated as we have become to consumerism and materialism, we do not easily grasp the beauty and power of a simple, unenslaved-to-buying-more-and-more-stuff life. We cannot imagine the freedom of genuine friendships that cross every line sin has built between people, especially the lines of class. I have come to believe that economic barriers are the hardest ones to overcome in forming genuine community in our culture. The money barrier is harder than racial reconciliation, or the full inclusion of LGBT friends in the life of the church.

By the time most of us are in our late twenties we have internalized the idea that sharing a common purse is absolutely

3. "Pope Chooses Simple Residence over Regal Papal Apartment," http://worldnews.nbcnews.com/_news/2013/03/26/17477922-pope-chooses-simple-residence-over-regal-papal-apartment?lite.

4. http://www.huffingtonpost.com/2013/03/28/pope-francis-holy-thursday-foot-washing_n_2972775.html.

anti-American and probably unChristian. It is more socially acceptable to describe one's sex life to strangers than to talk about one's money with friends. Telling others how much you earn is considered shameful and risky unless you are broke and need help, you are United Methodist clergy and you have no choice, or you are Warren Buffett and setting a good example for others.[5] Intentionally choosing downward mobility is considered social and economic suicide, guaranteeing that in your dotage you'll be out on the street.

Squirreling away money for long-term care insurance has become part of the norm for middle class America. We don't expect family members to take care of us as we age. The idea that our faith community would do it never occurs to us, partly because we are fickle and change churches when we get mad at the preacher. No, we expect to pay for our own care with long-term care insurance we have purchased for ourselves, in a designated facility we have chosen. Though this way of life is less than a hundred years old in America, we have come to think of it as normal, as just the way things are.

That this is not normal came home to me several years ago when I took my mother to get a pedicure at our neighborhood salon. Mary, the Vietnamese woman who owned the shop, chatted away as she gently trimmed and polished Mom's nails. I noticed that while Mary was brusque with my toes she treated Mom with something akin to reverence. When she found out that Mom had come to live with us because of health problems she stopped abruptly, blinking in astonishment. "Back home we take care parents," she blurted out. "We respect! Parents wise. Beautiful. Look at Mom! She beautiful. Americans not respect parents. Put away, not care, not respect," she said. "Mom!" she shouted, clutching my

5. UM Clergy salaries are published in the Annual Conference Journal every year. Every member of the local church knows how much his or her pastor earns. UM laity are under no obligation to tell the pastor how much they earn, lest there be uncomfortable expectations about tithes. Warren Buffett is a wildly successful businessman and philanthropist who has pledged to give away 99 percent of his wealth to make the world a better place. See http://en.wikipedia.org/wiki/Warren_Buffett.

mother's foot, "you very lucky live with daughter. You not American. You Vietnamese. Very, very lucky!" Waving the bottle of polish in my direction, Mary smiled beatifically. "You!" she said. "You Vietnamese daughter."

I did not know what to say. My mother lived with us for seven years, then when I began traveling a great deal with my work our family and Mom determined it was time for her to join my sisters and their families in Alaska. Mom said that with her health more stable she really wanted to return to living in her own apartment, to increase her sense of independence. But she wanted to be close enough to family to see one of us every day. She is in Alaska now, a five-minute walk from my sister's house, befriending everyone she meets and receiving a steady stream of visitors, including family who come every day. We are all now comfortable with her choice, though we worried a lot at the beginning. Her health had been very poor for several years. What if something happened? But we wanted to respect her wishes, so we helped her find the right place to live and the care support needed for her daily tasks.

Yet I must confess that of late I have been avoiding Mary. I don't want her to know Mom is in an apartment, even if it was Mom's decision. She will not understand Mom's American choice. I have lost my status as a Vietnamese daughter. Those toenail clippers are scary.

Subverting the Norms and Taking the Flak

Virtually every major component of residential, new monastic life is subversive of American norms about money and relationships. To choose to live in community, even if you do not share a common purse with all your income, is to have to shed the confining husk of materialism and consumerism that keeps us from living generously. To make this choice to live in community is to give up, day after day, the stranglehold that consumerism has on our affections. We need faithful guides who can help us find our way. This is part of the abbot's work.

There are also challenges related to individualism. In U.S. American culture individualism, high mobility, and the ideal of the nuclear (rather than extended) family seriously impact our experience *of* community. For many middle class children the most formative experiences in communal life are participation in organized sports. It is not uncommon for busy families to not eat meals together regularly because the pace of life is so fast. For many children who grow up in the suburbs the idea of knowing the people on your street and doing life together is downright foreign.

Add to this the number of broken and blended families, families with addictions, abuse, and other dysfunctions, as well as the general lack of skill in negotiating conflict or communicating clearly and directly, and most of us bring a simmering stew of disaster, with all our good intentions, when we gather into an intentional community. Failure of guidance is the biggest reason communities fail. We need help from those who have walked with Jesus for a long time.

What Does the Abbot Do?

The abbot guides the community in its formation, practice, and covenanted accountability for the three basic practices of prayer, hospitality, and missional service. A good abbot is deeply grounded in practices of prayer, is a person of profound hospitality, and has long experience with "resisting evil, oppression and injustice in whatever forms they present themselves," to use the language of baptismal vows.[6] In a best-case scenario she or he has training as a spiritual director, has pastoral gifts, is patient, discerning, wise, and has a great sense of humor. A good abbot above all else loves people.

In our communities Abbot Jerry Moore visits each of our houses two to three times per month, usually participating in a community meal and evening prayer. He thus is part of the

6. These vows are common to mainline traditions, including the United Methodist Church. See http://www.kintera.org/atf/cf/%7B3482e846-598f-460a-b9a7-386734470eda%7D/BAPTISMAL-RITUAL-REVISED.PDF.

ordinary flow of weekly activity. He gets to know all of the residents and their contexts and he forms good relationships with the anchor churches. He especially cultivates the formation of the house stewards with steward retreats and one-on-one care.[7] Because of all this relationship-building Jerry is able to help residents discern and faithfully live into their incarnational ministry in the neighborhood of their house.

In addition to his many years of experience as a pastor and spiritual director, Jerry has training and long experience in ministries of social justice. He understands the difference between works of mercy (addressing immediate symptoms of injustice such as hunger) and works of justice (addressing systemic causes of injustice such as unfair immigration law). He knows how complex poverty is, and how the church can either help to perpetuate poverty and injustice or bring about transformation. Because one element of the faithful abbot's work is mentoring, Jerry is teaching our residents how to live according to Micah 6:8: "He has told you, human one, what is good and what the Lord requires from you: to do justice, embrace faithful love, and walk humbly with your God."

Finally, the abbot must be emotionally healthy and be able to both practice and teach good communication and conflict resolution skills. For all the reasons already stated, guidance is necessary for most of us as we learn to embrace a lifestyle in which the wolf can lie down with the lamb, and a little child can lead them.[8] While Jerry does not live with the houses he guides, he also lives in intentional community at Adrian House, a residence of several older adults, four of whom are clergy and spiritual directors. Part of Jerry's credibility and authority in his role of abbot comes from his living the same kind of rhythms of prayer, hospitality, and missional service in intentional community.

7. House steward is the title we give to persons who facilitate the rhythms of life in each house. They also make sure the utility bills get paid!

8. Here I am referring to the extraordinary beauty of Edward Hicks's paintings depicting Isaiah 11:6, the promise of God's power to bring about peaceful community among persons and nations that have always been enemies. See http://www.worcesterart.org/Collection/American/1934.65.html.

But where can one find a good abbot? Is there a retired clergy or layperson in your circles who has the kind of gifts, wisdom, and experience described above? Is there an older person who has been a vibrant Christian for a long time, who is already fruitful at mentoring young adults? In cities like Chicago where there are several new monastic communities that have been around for decades, someone with years of experience living in community may be willing to serve in this role for your newly forming community. This guidance could be provided on the ground or across great distances through video chat.

Even if you cannot find the right person who would be in the abbot role at the beginning of your community's journey, you can find conversation partners online through networks of new monastic communities[9] so that you have the benefit of conversation, feedback, and guidance as your group begins to coalesce. No matter what, pray and look for persons who can companion your community in wisdom and love.

For Reflection:

Describe someone who has been an abba or amma in your life, especially when you were a young Christian. How did you come to know this person? How did they relate to you? What are some gifts that you carry with you today because of the time and love they invested in you?

---

9. On the New Monasticism website simply click on "Find Us" to go to the page titled "Community of Communities." There you can locate new monastic communities in your area. See http://www.communityofcommunities.info. Most new monastic folk are happy to share their stories and offer insight to others who are forming communities.

Recommended Readings for Missional, New Monastic and Emerging Church Contexts

Bret Wells

Missional

Academic and Foundational Texts

Bosch, David J. *Transforming Mission: Paradigm Shifts in Theology of Mission.* Maryknoll, NY: Orbis, 1991.

Chilcote, Paul W., and Laceye C. Warner. *The Study of Evangelism: Exploring a Missional Practice of the Church.* Grand Rapids: Eerdmans, 2008.

Gibbs, Eddie. *Church Morph: How Megatrends are Reshaping Christian Communities.* Grand Rapids: Baker Academic, 2009.

Grenz, Stanley J. *Theology for the Community of God.* Grand Rapids: Eerdmans, 2000.

Guder, Darrell. *Be My Witness: The Church's Mission, Message, and Messengers.* Grand Rapids: Eerdmans, 1985.

———.*The Continuing Conversion of the Church.* Grand Rapids: Eerdmans, 2000.

——— "Missional Hermeneutics: The Missional Authority of Scripture." *Mission Focus,* Annual Review, 15 (2007) 106–21. (PDF version: http://www.ambs.edu/publishing/documents/MissionFocus.

———. "Missional Hermeneutics: The Missional Vocation of the Congregation—and How Scripture Shapes That Calling." *Mission Focus,* Annual Review, 15 (2007) 125–42.

Guder, Darrell, and Lois Barrett. *Missional Church: A Vision for the Sending of the Church in North America.* Grand Rapids: Eerdmans, 1998.

Hastings, Ross. *Missional God, Missional Church: Hope for Re-evangelizing the West.* Downers Grove, IL: IVP Academic, 2012.

Hirsch, Alan. *The Forgotten Ways: Reactivating the Missional Church.* Grand Rapids: Brazos, 2006.

Hunsberger, George R. "Proposals for a Missional Hermeneutic." The Gospel and Our Culture Network Newsletter, eseries no. 2, January 28, 2009. http://www.gocn.org/resources/newsletters/2009/01/gospel-and-our-culture.

Hunsberger, George, and Craig Van Gelder. *The Church Between Gospel and Culture: The Emerging Mission in North America.* Grand Rapids: Eerdmans, 1996.

Newbigin, Lesslie. *Foolishness to the Greeks: The Gospel and Western Culture.* Grand Rapids: Eerdmans, 1986.

————. *The Gospel in a Pluralist Society.* Grand Rapids: Eerdmans, 1989.

————. *The Open Secret: An Introduction to the Theology of Mission.* Rev. ed. Grand Rapids: Eerdmans, 1995.

————. *Signs Amid the Rubble: The Purpose of God in Human History.* Edited by Geoffrey Wainwright. Grand Rapids: Eerdmans, 2003.

Ross, Maggie. *Pillars of Flame: Power, Priesthood, and Spiritual Maturity.* New York: Seabury, 1988, 2007.

Woodward, J. R. *Creating a Missional Culture: Equipping the Church for the Sake of the World.* Downers Grove, IL: InterVarsity, 2012.

Wright, Christopher J. H. *The Mission of God: Unlocking the Bible's Grand Narrative.* Downers Grove, IL: InterVarsity, 2006.

————. *The Mission of God's People: A Biblical Theology of the Church's Mission.* Grand Rapids: Zondervan, 2010.

Leading Contemporary Voices in the Missional Conversation

Breen, Mike. *Leading Kingdom Movements: The "Everyman" Notebook on How to Change the World.* Pawleys Island, SC: 3DM, 2013.

Breen, Mike, and Alex Absalom. *Launching Missional Communities: A Field Guide.* Pawleys Island, SC: 3DM, 2010.

Breen, Mike, and Steve Cockram. *Building a Discipling Culture.* Grand Rapids: Zondervan, 2009.

Breen, Mike, and Jon Tyson. *Multiplying Missional Leaders: From Half-hearted Volunteers to a Mobilized Kingdom Force.* Pawleys Island, SC: 3DM, 2012.

Cole, Neil. *Church 3.0: Upgrades for the Future of the Church.* San Francisco: Jossey-Bass, 2010.

————. *Organic Church: Growing Faith Where Life Happens.* San Francisco: Jossey-Bass, 2005.

————. *Organic Leadership: Leading Naturally Right Where You Are.* Grand Rapids: Baker, 2009.

Fitch, David. *The Great Giveaway: Reclaiming the Mission of the Church from Big Business, Parachurch Organizations, Psychotherapy, Consumer Capitalism, and Other Modern Maladies.* Grand Rapids: Baker, 2005.

———. *The End of Evangelicalism? Discerning a New Faithfulness for Mission; Towards an Evangelical Political Theology.* Eugene, OR: Cascade, 2011.

Fitch, David, and Geoff Holsclaw. *Prodigal Christianity: 10 Signposts into the Missional Frontier.* San Francisco: Jossey-Bass, 2013.

Frost, Michael. *Exiles: Living Missionally in a Post-Christian Culture.* Peabody, MA: Hendrickson, 2006.

———. *The Road to Missional: Journey to the Center of the Church.* Grand Rapids: Baker, 2011.

Frost, Michael, and Alan Hirsch. *The Faith of Leap: Embracing a Theology of Risk, Adventure and Courage.* Grand Rapids: Baker, 2011.

———. *The Shaping of Things to Come: Innovation and Mission for the 21st-Century Church.* Grand Rapids: Baker, 2003.

Halter, Hugh and Matt Smay. *And: The Gathered and Scattered Church.* Grand Rapids: Zondervan, 2010.

——— *The Tangible Kingdom: Creating Incarnational Community.* San Francisco: Josey-Bass, 2008.

——— *The Tangible Kingdom Primer: An 8-Week Guide to Incarnational Community.* Anaheim, CA: CRM Empowering Leaders, 2009.

Hatmaker, Brandon. *Barefoot Church: Serving the Least in a Consumer Culture.* Grand Rapids: Zondervan, 2011.

Hirsch, Alan, and Darryn Altclass. *The Forgotten Ways Handbook: A Practical Guide for Developing Missional Churches.* Grand Rapids: Brazos, 2009.

Hirsch, Alan, and Tim Catchim. *The Permanent Revolution: Apostolic Imagination and Practice for the 21st-Century Church.* San Francisco: Jossey-Bass, 2012.

Hirsch, Alan, and Dave Ferguson. *On The Verge: A Journey Into the Apostolic Future of the Church.* Grand Rapids: Zondervan, 2011.

Hirsch, Alan, and Lance Ford. *Right Here Right Now: Everyday Mission for Everyday People.* Grand Rapids: Baker, 2011.

Hirsch, Alan, and Michael Frost. *ReJesus: A Wild Messiah for a Missional Church.* Peabody, MA: Hendrickson, 2009.

Hirsch, Alan, and Debra Hirsch. *Untamed: Reactivating a Missional Form of Discipleship.* Grand Rapids: Baker, 2010.

Huckins, Jon and Rob Yackley. *Thin Places: Six Postures for Creating and Practicing Missional Community.* Kansas City, MO: The House Studio, 2012.

McNeal, Reggie. *Missional Renaissance: Changing the Scorecard for the Church.* San Francisco: Josey-Bass, 2009.

———. *The Present Future: Six Tough Questions for the Church.* San Francisco: Jossey-Bass, 2009.

———. *Missional Communities: The Rise of the Post-Congregational Church.* San Francisco: Jossey-Bass, 2011.

Roxburgh, Alan. *Introducing the Missional Church: What It Is, Why It Matters, How to Become One.* Grand Rapids: Baker, 2009.

———. *Missional: Joining God in the Neighborhood.* Grand Rapids: Baker, 2011.

———. *The Missional Leader: Equipping Your Church to Reach a Changing World.* San Francisco: Jossey-Bass, 2006.

Scandrette, Mark. *Practicing the Way of Jesus: Life Together in the Kingdom of Love.* Downers Grove, IL: InterVarsity, 2011.

Stetzer, Ed. *Planting Missional Churches.* Nashville: Broadman & Holman, 2006.

Stetzer, Ed, and Phillip Nation. *Compelled by Love: The Most Excellent Way to Missional Living.* Birmingham, AL: New Hope, 2008.

Stetzer, Ed, and David Putman. *Breaking the Missional Code: Your Church Can Become a Missionary in Your Community.* Nashville: Broadman & Holman, 2006.

Van Gelder, Craig. *Ministry of the Missional Church: A Community Led by the Spirit.* Grand Rapids: Baker, 2007.

———. *The Missional Church and Denominations: Helping Congregations Develop a Missional Identity.* Grand Rapids: Eerdmans, 2008.

———. *The Missional Church in Context: Helping Congregations Develop Contextual Ministry.* Grand Rapids: Eerdmans, 2007.

Van Gelder, Craig, and Dwight Zscheile. *Missional Church in Perspective: Mapping Trends and Shaping the Conversation.* Grand Rapids: Baker Academic, 2011.

Viola, Frank. *Finding Organic Church: A Comprehensive Guide to Starting and Sustaining Authentic Christian Communities.* Colorado Springs: David C. Cook, 2009.

———. *Reimagining Church: Pursuing the Dream of Organic Christianity.* Colorado Springs: David C. Cook, 2008.

Zscheile, Dwight J. *People of the Way: Renewing Episcopal Identity.* New York: Morehouse, 2012.

Additional Missional Texts

Addison, Steve. *What Jesus Started: Joining the Movement, Changing the World.* Downers Grove, IL: InterVarsity, 2012.

Denison, Charles. *Mainline Manifesto: The Inevitable New Church.* St. Louis: Chalice, 2005.

Helland, Roger and Leonard Hjalmarson. *Missional Spirituality: Embodying God's Love from the Inside Out.* Downers Grove, IL: InterVarsity, 2011.

Hunter, Todd. *Christianity Beyond Belief: Following Jesus for the Sake of Others.* Downers Grove, IL: InterVarsity, 2009.

Mancini, Will. *Church Unique: How Missional Leaders Cast Vision, Capture Culture and Create Movement.* San Francisco: Jossey-Bass, 2008.

McKnight, John, and Peter Block. *The Abundant Community: Awakening the Power of Families and Neighborhoods.* San Francisco: Berrett-Koehler, 2010.

Oldenburg, Ray. *The Great Good Place: Cafes, Coffee Shops, Bookstores, Bars, Hair Salons, and Other Hangouts at the Heart of the Community.* New York: Marlowe & Company, 1999.

Pathak, Jay and Dave Runyon. *The Art of Neighboring: Building Genuine Relationships Right Outside Your Door.* Grand Rapids: Baker, 2012.

Smith, C. Christopher. *Growing Deeper in Our Church Communities: 50 Ideas for Connection in a Disconnected Age.* Indianapolis: Englewood Review of Books, 2010. Kindle.

Swanson, Eric and Sam Williams. *To Transform a City: Whole Church, Whole Gospel, Whole City.* Grand Rapids: Zondervan, 2010.

Zimmerman, David A. *Deliver Us from Me-Ville.* Colorado Springs: David C. Cook, 2008.

Zscheile, Dwight, ed. *Cultivating Sent Communities: Missional Spiritual Formation.* Grand Rapids: Eerdmans, 2012.

Emerging Church Contexts

Anderson, Ray. *An Emergent Theology for Emerging Churches.* Downers Grove, IL: InterVarsity, 2006.

Bell, Rob. *Sex God: Exploring the Endless Connections Between Sexuality and Spirituality.* Grand Rapids: Zondervan, 2007.

———. *Velvet Elvis: Repainting the Christian Faith.* Grand Rapids: Zondervan, 2005.

Bell, Rob, and Don Golden. *Jesus Wants to Save Christians: A Manifesto for the Church in Exile.* Grand Rapids: Zondervan, 2008.

Bolger, Ryan K. *The Gospel after Christendom: New Voices, New Cultures, New Expressions.* Grand Rapids: Baker Academic, 2012.

Caputo, John D. *What Would Jesus Deconstruct? The Good News of Postmodernism for the Church.* Grand Rapids: Baker Academic, 2007.

Gibbs, Eddie, and Ryan K. Bolger. *Emerging Churches: Creating Christian Community in Postmodern Cultures.* Grand Rapids: Baker Academic, 2005.

Gray-Reeves, Mary and Michael Perham. *The Hospitality of God: Emerging Worship for a Missional Church.* New York: Seabury, 2011.

Frambach, Nathan. *Emerging Ministry: Being Church Today.* Minneapolis: Augsburg Fortress, 2007.

Jones, Tony. *The Church Is Flat: The Relational Ecclesiology of the Emerging Church Movement.* Minneapolis: The JoPa Group, 2011.

Keel, Tim. *Intuitive Leadership: Embracing a Paradigm of Narrative, Metaphor, and Chaos.* Grand Rapids: Baker, 2007.

Recommended Readings

Kimball, Dan. *The Emerging Church: Vintage Christianity for New Generations.* Grand Rapids: Zondervan, 2003.

―――. *They Like Jesus, But Not the Church: Insights from Emerging Generations.* Grand Rapids: Zondervan, 2007.

Kinnaman, Dave. *You Lost Me: Why Young Christians Are Leaving Church. . .and Rethinking Faith.* Grand Rapids: Baker, 2011.

McLaren, Brian. *The Church on the Other Side: Doing Ministry in the Postmodern Matrix.* Rev. ed. Grand Rapids: Zondervan, 2000.

―――. *Everything Must Change: When the World's Biggest Problems and Jesus' Good News Collide.* Nashville: Thomas Nelson, 2007.

―――. *Finding Our Way Again: The Return of the Ancient Practices.* Nashville: Thomas Nelson, 2008.

―――. *A Generous Orthodoxy: Why I Am a Missional, Evangelical, Post/ Protestant, Liberal/Conservative, Mystical/Poetic, Biblical, Charismatic/ Contemplative, Fundamentalist/Calvinist, Anabaptist/Anglican, Methodist, Catholic, Green, Incarnational, Depressed-yet-Hopeful, Emergent, Unfinished Christian.* Grand Rapids: Zondervan, 2004.

―――. *The Last Word and The Word After That: A Tale of Faith, Doubt, and a New Kind of Christianity.* San Francisco: Jossey-Bass, 2005.

―――. *More Ready Than You Realize: Evangelism and Dance in the Postmodern Matrix.* Grand Rapids: Zondervan, 2002.

―――. *A New Kind of Christian: A Tale of Two Friends on a Spiritual Journey.* San Francisco: Jossey-Bass, 2001.

―――. *The Story We Find Ourselves In: Further Adventures of a New Kind of Christian.* San Francisco: Jossey-Bass, 2003.

―――. *A New Kind of Christianity: Ten Questions That are Transforming the Church.* New York: HarperCollins, 2010.

―――. *The Secret Message of Jesus: Uncovering the Truth That Could Change Everything.* Nashville: Thomas Nelson, 2006.

―――. *Naked Spirituality: A Life with God in 12 Simple Words.* New York: HarperCollins, 2011.

―――. *Why Did Jesus, Moses, the Buddha, and Mohammed Cross the Road? Christian Identity in a Multi-Faith World.* New York: Jericho Books, 2012.

McLaren, Brian, and Tony Campolo. *Adventures in Missing the Point: How the Culture-Controlled Church Neutered the Gospel.* Grand Rapids: Zondervan, 2003.

McKnight, Scott, Peter Rollins, Kevin Corcoran, and Jason Clark. *Church in the Present Tense: A Candid Look at What's Emerging.* Grand Rapids: Brazos, 2011.

Pagitt, Doug. *Church ReImagined: The Spiritual Formation of People in Communities of Faith.* Grand Rapids: Zondervan, 2003.

Rollins, Peter. *How (Not) to Speak of God.* Brewster, MA: Paraclete, 2006.

―――. *The Fidelity of Betrayal: Towards a Church Beyond Belief.* Brewster, MA: Paraclete, 2008.

———— *Insurrection: To Believe is Human; To Doubt, Divine.* New York: Howard, 2011.

————. *The Idolatry of God: Breaking Our Addiction to Certainty and Satisfaction.* New York: Howard, 2011.

Snider, Phil, ed. *The Hyphenateds: How Emergence Christianity is Re-Traditioning Mainline Practices.* St. Louis: Chalice, 2011.

Sweet, Leonard. *The Gospel According to Starbucks: Living With a Grande Passion.* Colorado Springs: Waterbrook, 2007.

Tickle, Phyllis. *The Great Emergence: How Christianity is Changing and Why.* Grand Rapids: Baker, 2008.

————. *Emergence Christianity: What It Is, Where It Is Going, and Why It Matters.* Grand Rapids: Baker Books, 2012.

Webber, Robert. *The Younger Evangelicals: Facing the Challenges of a New World.* Grand Rapids: Baker Books, 2002.

New Monastic & Intentional Community

Alexander, John F. *Being Church: Reflections on How to Live as the People of God.* Eugene, OR: Cascade, 2012.

Arpin-Ricci, Jamie. *The Cost of Community: Jesus, St. Francis and Life in the Kingdom.* Downers Grove, IL: InterVarsity, 2011.

Bessenecker, Scott. *Living Mission: The Vision and Voices of the New Friars.* Downers Grove, IL: InterVarsity, 2010.

————. *The New Friars: The Emerging Movement Serving the World's Poor.* Downers Grove, IL: InterVarsity, 2006.

Bonhoeffer, Dietrich. *Life Together.* San Francisco: Harper & Row, 1954.

Claiborne, Shane. *Irresistible Revolution: Living as an Ordinary Radical.* Grand Rapids: Zondervan, 2006.

Claiborne, Shane, and Chris Haw. *Jesus For President: Politics for Ordinary Radicals.* Grand Rapids: Zondervan, 2008.

Claiborne, Shane, and John Perkins. *Follow Me to Freedom: Leading as an Ordinary Radical.* Ventura, CA: Regal, 2009.

Claiborne, Shane, and Jonathan Wilson-Hartgrove. *Becoming the Answer to Our Prayers: Prayer for Ordinary Radicals.* Downers Grove, IL: InterVarsity, 2008.

Chester, Tim, and Steve Timmis. *Total Church: A Radical Reshaping Around Gospel and Community.* Wheaton, IL: Crossway, 2008.

Cray, Graham, Ian Mobsby, and Aaron Kennedy, eds. *Ancient Faith, Future Mission: New Monasticism as Fresh Expression of Church.* London: Canterbury, 2010.

Duggins, Larry. *Simple Harmony: Thoughts on Holistic Christian Life.* n.p.: Columkille, 2012.

Freeman, Andy. *Punk Monk: New Monasticism and the Ancient Art of Breathing.* Ventura, CA: Regal, 2007.

Heath, Elaine, and Scott Kisker. *Longing for Spring: A New Vision for Wesleyan Community.* Eugene, OR: Pickwick, 2010.

Jacobsen, Wayne, and Clay Jacobsen. *Authentic Relationships: Discover the Lost Art of "One Anothering."* Grand Rapids: Baker, 2003.

Janzen, David. *The Intentional Christian Community Handbook: For Idealists, Hypocrites, and Wannabe Disciples of Jesus.* Brewster, MA: Paraclete, 2013.

Kauffman, Ivan J. *Follow Me: A History of Christian Intentionality.* Eugene, OR: Cascade, 2009.

Longenecker, Richard N., ed. *Community Formation: In the Early Church and in the Church Today.* Peabody, MA: Hendrickson, 2002.

McQuiston, John II. *Always We Begin Again: The Benedictine Way of Living.* Harrisburg, PA: Morehouse, 1996.

Mobsby, Ian, and Mark Berry. *A New Monastic Handbook: From Vision to Practice.* London: Canterbury, 2013.

Okholm, Dennis L. *Monk Habits for Everyday People: Benedictine Spirituality for Protestants.* Grand Rapids: Brazos, 2007.

Stock, Jon, Tim Otto, and Jonathan Wilson-Hartgrove. *Inhabiting the Church: Biblical Wisdom for a New Monasticism.* Eugene, OR: Cascade, 2007.

Perkins, John. *With Justice for All: A Strategy for Community Development.* Ventura, CA: Regal, 2007.

Rutba House, ed. *School(s) for Conversion: 12 Marks of New Monasticism.* Eugene, OR: Cascade, 2005.

Sanders, Brian. *In Your Underwear: Life in Intentional Christian Community.* n.p.: Underground Media, 2011.

———. *Life After Church: God's Call to Disillusioned Christians.* Downers Grove, IL: InterVarsity, 2007.

Sine, Tom. *The New Conspirators: Creating the Future One Mustard Seed at a Time.* Downers Grove, IL: InterVarsity, 2008.

Wilson, Jonathan R. *Living Faithfully in a Fragmented World: From 'After Virtue' to a New Monasticism,* 2nd ed. Eugene, OR: Cascade, 2010.

Wilson-Hartgrove, Jonathan. *The Awakening of Hope: Why We Practice a Common Faith.* Grand Rapids: Zondervan, 2012.

———. *Free to be Bound: Church Beyond the Color Line.* Colorado Springs: NavPress, 2008.

———. *God's Economy: Redefining the Health and Wealth Gospel.* Grand Rapids: Zondervan, 2009.

———. *New Monasticism: What It Has to Say to Today's Church.* Grand Rapids: Brazos, 2008.

———. *The Wisdom of Stability: Rooting Faith in a Mobile Culture.* Brewster, MA: Paraclete, 2010.

Practical Theology for Emerging Contexts

Beck, Richard. *Unclean: Meditations on Purity, Hospitality, and Mortality.* Eugene, OR: Cascade, 2011.

Bass, Diana Butler. *The Practicing Congregation: Imagining a New Old Church.* Herndon, VA: Alban Institute, 2004.

Bloesch, Donald G. *Spirituality Old and New: Recovering Authentic Spiritual Life.* Downers Grove, IL: IVP Academic, 2007.

Claiborne, Shane, Jonathan Wilson-Hartgrove, and Enuma Okoro. *Common Prayer: A Liturgy for Ordinary Radicals.* Grand Rapids: Zondervan, 2010.

Corbett, Steve and Brian Fikkert. *When Helping Hurts: How to Alleviate Poverty Without Hurting the Poor . . . and Yourself.* Chicago: Moody, 2009.

Donovan, Vincent. *Christianity Rediscovered.* Maryknoll, NY: Orbis, 1978.

Everts, Don, and Doug Schaupp. *I Once Was Lost: What Postmodern Skeptics Taught Us About Their Path to Jesus.* Downers Grove, IL: InterVarsity, 2008.

Farley, Edward. *Practicing Gospel: Unconventional Thoughts on the Church's Ministry.* Louisville: Westminster John Knox, 2003.

Ford, Leighton. *The Attentive Life: Discerning God's Presence in All Things.* Downers Grove, IL: InterVarsity, 2008.

Frazee, Randy. *The Connecting Church: Beyond Small Groups to Authentic Community.* Grand Rapids: Zondervan, 2001.

Geiger, Eric, Michael Kelley, and Philip Nation. *Transformational Discipleship: How People Really Grow.* Nashville: Broadman & Holman, 2012.

Guenther, Margaret. *At Home in the World: A Rule of Life for the Rest of Us.* New York: Seabury, 2006.

Halter, Hugh. *Sacrilege: Finding Life in the Unorthodox Way of Jesus.* Grand Rapids: Baker, 2011.

Heath, Elaine. *The Mystic Way of Evangelism: A Contemplative Vision for Christian Outreach.* Grand Rapids: Baker Academic, 2008.

———. *Naked Faith: The Mystical Theology of Phoebe Palmer.* Eugene, OR: Pickwick, 2009.

Highfield, Ron. *God, Freedom and Human Dignity: Embracing a God-Centered Identity in a Me-Centered Culture.* Downers Grove, IL: InterVarsity, 2013.

Hunter, George III. *The Celtic Way of Evangelism: How Christianity Can Reach the West . . . Again.* Nashville: Abingdon, 2000.

Jones, Tony. *Soul Shaper: Exploring Spirituality and Contemplative Practices in Youth Ministry.* Grand Rapids: Zondervan, 2003.

Kallenberg, Brad. *Live to Tell: Evangelism in a Postmodern Age.* Grand Rapids: Brazos, 2002.

Liederbach, Mark and Alvin L. Reid. *The Convergent Church: Missional Worshippers in an Emerging Culture.* Grand Rapids: Kregel, 2009.

MacDonald, Glenn. *The Disciple-Making Church: From Dry Bones to Spiritual Vitality.* Grand Haven, MI: FaithWalk, 2004.

McKnight, Scot. *A Community Called Atonement.* Nashville: Abingdon, 2007.

———. *The King Jesus Gospel: The Original Good News Revisited.* Grand Rapids: Zondervan, 2011.

———. *Praying With the Church: Following Jesus Daily, Hourly, Today.* Brewster, MA: Paraclete, 2006.

McNeil, Brenda Salter. *A Credible Witness: Reflections on Power, Evangelism and Race.* Downers Grove, IL: InterVarsity, 2008.

Medearis, Carl. *Speaking of Jesus: The Art of Not-Evangelism.* Colorado Springs: David C. Cook, 2011.

Moltmann, Jürgen. *The Trinity and the Kingdom: The Doctrine of God.* Minneapolis: Fortress, 1993.

Norris, Kristopher. *Pilgrim Practices: Discipleship for a Missional Church.* Eugene, OR: Cascade, 2012.

Ogden, Greg. *Transforming Discipleship: Making Disciples a Few at a Time.* Downers Grove, IL: InterVarsity, 2003.

———. *Unfinished Business: Return the Ministry to the People of God.* Rev. ed. Grand Rapids: Zondervan, 2003.

Pagitt, Doug. *Preaching ReImagined: The Role of the Sermon in Communities of Faith.* Grand Rapids: Zondervan, 2005.

Pohl, Christine D. *Making Room: Recovering Hospitality as a Christian Tradition.* Grand Rapids: Eerdmans, 1999.

Rainer, Thom S. and Eric Geiger. *Simple Church: Returning to God's Process for Making Disciples.* Nashville: Broadman & Holman, 2006.

Rieger, Joerg. *God and The Excluded: Visions and Blindspots in Contemporary Theology.* Minneapolis: Fortress, 2001.

———. *No Rising Tide: Theology, Economics, and the Future.* Minneapolis: Fortress, 2009.

Rieger, Joerg, ed. *Theology From the Belly of the Whale: A Frederick Herzog Reader.* Harrisburg, PA: Trinity Press International, 1999.

Schmit, Clayton J. *Sent and Gathered: A Worship Manual for the Missional Church.* Grand Rapids: Baker Academic, 2009.

Smay, Matt. *Transcend: Beyond the Limits of Discipleship.* Littleton, CO: Missio, 2013.

Stearns, Richard. *The Hole in Our Gospel: What Does God Expect of Us? The Answer That Changed My Life and Might Just Change the World.* Nashville: Thomas Nelson, 2009.

Stone, Bryan P. *Evangelism After Christendom: The Theology and Practice of Christian Witness.* Grand Rapids: Brazos, 2006.

Vanhoozer, Kevin J., Charles A. Anderson, and Michael J. Sleasman, eds. *Everyday Theology: How to Read Cultural Texts and Interpret Trends.* Grand Rapids: Baker Academic, 2007.

Volf, Miroslav. *In Our Likeness: The Church as the Image of the Trinity.* Grand Rapids: Eerdmans, 1998.

Webber, Robert E. *Ancient-Future Evangelism: Making Your Church a Faith-Forming Community.* Grand Rapids: Baker, 2003.

————. *Ancient-Future Faith: Rethinking Evangelicalism for a Postmodern World*. Grand Rapids: Baker, 1999.

————. *Ancient-Future Time: Forming Spirituality Through the Christian Year*. Grand Rapids: Baker, 2004.

————. *Journey to Jesus: The Worship, Evangelism, and Nurture Mission of the Church*. Nashville: Abingdon, 2001.

Wright, N. T. *Evil and the Justice of God*. Downers Grove, IL: InterVarsity, 2006.

————. *How God Became King: The Forgotten Story of the Gospels*. New York: HarperOne, 2012.

————. *Justification: God's Plan and Paul's Vision*. Downers Grove, IL: IVP Academic, 2009.

————. *Simply Christian: Why Christianity Makes Sense*. New York: HarperOne, 2006.

————. *Simply Jesus: A New Vision of Who He Was, What He Did, and Why He Matters*. New York: HarperOne, 2011.

————. *Surprised By Hope: Rethinking Heaven, the Resurrection, and the Mission of the Church*. New York: HarperOne, 2008.

Yaconelli, Mark. *Contemplative Youth Ministry: Practicing the Presence of Jesus*. Grand Rapids: Zondervan, 2006.

Yoder, John Howard. *Body Politics: Five Practices of the Christian Community Before the Watching World*. Scottdale, PA: Herald, 2001.

————. *The Politics of Jesus*. 2nd ed. Grand Rapids: Eerdmans, 1994.

Coaching for Leadership Development and Ministry in Missional Contexts

Collins, Gary R. *Christian Coaching: Helping Others Turn Potential into Reality*. Rev. ed. Colorado Springs: NavPress, 2009.

Crane, Thomas G. *The Heart of Coaching: Using Transformational Coaching to Create a High-Performance Coaching Culture*. 4th ed. San Diego: FTA Press, 2012.

Hargrove, Robert. *Masterful Coaching*. 3rd ed. San Francisco: Jossey-Bass, 2008.

Jackson, Paul Z. and Mark McKergow. *The Solutions Focus: Making Coaching & Change SIMPLE*. 2nd ed. Boston: Nicholas Brealey, 2012.

Kimsey-House, Henry, Karen Kimsey-House, Phillip Sandahl, and Laura Whitworth. *Co-Active Coaching: Changing Business, Transforming Lives*. 3rd ed. Boston: Nicholas Brealey, 2011.

Logan, Robert E., and Sherilyn Carlton. *Coaching 101: Discover the Power of Coaching*. St. Charles, IL: Church Smart Resources, 2003.

Szabo, Peter, and Daniel Meier. *Coaching Plain & Simple: Solution-Focused Coaching Essentials*. New York: Norton, 2008.

Melander, Rochelle. *A Generous Presence: Spiritual Leadership and the Art of Coaching*. Herndon, VA:Alban Institute, 2006.

Recommended Readings

Ogne, Steve and Tim Roehl. *Transformissional Coaching: Empowering Leaders in a Changing Ministry World.* Nashville: Broadman & Holman, 2008.

Stoltzfus, Tony. *The Calling Journey: Mapping the Stages of a Leader's Life Call; A Coaching Guide.* Redding, CA: Coach22 Bookstore, 2010.

———. *Coaching Questions: A Coach's Guide to Powerful Asking Skills.* Virginia Beach, VA: Tony Stoltzfus, 2008.

———. *Leadership Coaching: The Disciplines, Skills and Heart of a Christian Coach.* Virginia Beach, VA: Tony Stoltzfus, 2005.

Webb, Keith E. *The COACH Model for Christian Leaders: Powerful Leadership Skills for Solving Problems, Reaching Goals, & Developing Others.* Bellevue, WA: Active Results, 2012.

Whitmore, John. *Coaching for Performance: GROWing Human Potential and Purpose; The Principles and Practice of Coaching and Leadership.* 4th ed. Boston: Nicholas Brealey, 2013.

Works Cited

Aleshire, Daniel. "2021: A Theological Odyssey." A lecture delivered at a symposium on theological education, Pittsburgh, March, 2013.

Aquaponics and Earth Sustainable Living. http://www.aquaponicsandearth. org.

Base Communities. http://en.wikipedia.org/wiki/Christian_base_communities.

Bradshaw, John. http://www.johnbradshaw.com/healingtheshamethatbindsyou 1hourlecture.aspx.

Breen, Michael, and Alex Absalom. *Launching Missional Communities.* Pawleys Island, SC: Mike Breen/3DM, 2010.

Buchanan, Marguerite. Mercy Center, Burlingame, CA, workshop on truth-telling, relationships, and justice.

Buffet, Warren. http://en.wikipedia.org/wiki/Warren_Buffett.

Bush, Andrew. *Learning from the Least.* Eugene, OR: Cascade, 2013.

Butler Bass, Diana. *Christianity after Religion: The End of Church and the Birth of a New Spiritual Awakening.* New York: HarperOne, 2012.

———. *A People's History of Christianity: The Other Side of the Story.* New York: HarperCollins. 2009.

Claiborne, Shane. *Irresistible Revolution: Living as an Ordinary Radical.* Grand Rapids: Zondervan, 2006.

Claiborne, Shane, Jonathan Wilson-Hartgrove and Enuma Okoro. *Common Prayer: A Liturgy for Ordinary Radicals.* Grand Rapids: Zondervan, 2010.

Co-housing Movement in the United States. http://www.cohousing.org/what_ is_cohousing.

Communities of L'Arche. http://www.larcheusa.org/who-we-are/communities/.

Community of Communities. http://www.communityofcommunities.info.

Dunn, Elizabeth, and Michael Norton. *Happy Money: The Science of Smarter Spending.* New York: Simon and Schuster, 2013.

Ferguson, Ron, and George MacLeod. *The Iona Community.* Glasgow: Wild Goose, 2004.

Global Theological Education. http://www.smu.edu/Perkins/FacultyAcademics/ Global, Eighteenth Avenue Peace House. http://18thavepeacehouse.org.

Halter, Hugh, and Matt Smay. *Tangible Kingdom: Creating Incarnational Community*. San Francisco: Jossey-Bass, 2008.

Heath, Elaine A. *The Mystic Way of Evangelism: A Contemplative Vision for Christian Outreach*. Grand Rapids: Baker Academic, 2008.

Heath, Elaine A., and Scott Kisker. *Longing for Spring: A New Vision for Wesleyan Community*. Eugene, OR: Pickwick, 2010.

Hicks, Edward. Peaceable Kingdom. http://www.worcesterart.org/Collection/American/1934.65.html.

Hirsch, Alan. *The Forgotten Ways*. Grand Rapids: Brazos, 2006.

Homestead Heritage. http://www.homesteadheritage.com.

Janzen, David. *The Intentional Community Handbook: For Idealists, Hypocrites, and Wannabe Disciples of Jesus*. Brewster, MA: Paraclete, 2013.

Jim Jones History. http://en.wikipedia.org/wiki/Jim_Jones.

Kibbutz. http://www.kibbutz.org.il/eng/.

Linn, Dennis, and Shelia Fabricant Linn and Matthew Linn. *Sleeping with Bread*. Mahwah, NJ: Paulist, 1995.

Matheson, Peter, ed. *Reformation Christianity*. A People's History of Christianity, vol. 5. Minneapolis: Fortress, 2007.

Monty Python and the Holy Grail. Terry Gilliam and Terry Jones, directors. Michael White Productions, 1975.

New Day, Epworth Project, and the Academy. www.missionalwisdom.com.

New Day Rule of Life and Covenant Questions. www.missionalwisdom.com/new-day/rule-of-life.

New Monasticism. http://www.newmonasticism.org/weekend.php.

Ninety-five Theses. en.wikipedia.org/wiki/The_Ninety-Five_Theses.

Nouwen, Henri. *Life of the Beloved: Spiritual Living in a Secular World*. New York: Crossroads, 2002.

Nouwen, Henri. *The Wounded Healer*. New York: Image, 1979.

Obama, Barak. Speech to United Nations Assembly, September 25, 2012. http://www.guardian.co.uk/world/2012/sep/25/obama-un-general-assembly-transcript.

Oregon Extension. http://oregonextension.org/.

Outward Bound. http://www.outwardbound.org.

Plowpoint. www.plowpoint.org.

"Pope Chooses Simple Residence over Regal Papal Apartment." http://worldnews.nbcnews.com/_news/2013/03/26/17477922-pope-chooses-simple-residence-over-regal-papal-apartment?lite.

Pope Francis. http://www.huffingtonpost.com/2013/03/28/pope-francis-holy-thursday-foot-washing_n_2972775.html.

Rieger, Joerg. *Christ and Empire: From Paul to Postcolonial Times*. Minneapolis: Fortress, 2007.

Riess, Jana. "Redefining Retirement: A Conversation with Walter Brueggmann." www.religionnews.com/blogs/jana-riess/redefining-retirement-a-conversation-with-walter-brueggemann.

Rohr, Richard. "The Franciscan Alternative Orthodoxy." *The Mendicant*, vol. 3. no. 2 (Summer 2013) 1.

―――. *The Naked Now: Learning to See as the Mystics See*. New York: Crossroad, 2009.

Roxburgh, Alan J. and Scott Boren. *Introducing the Missional Church: What It Is, Why It Matters, How to Become One*. Grand Rapids: Baker, 2009.

Rutba House, eds. *School(s) for Conversion: 12 Marks of the New Monasticism*. Eugene, OR: Cascade, 2005.

Spener, Jacob. *Pia Desideria*. http://www.ctlibrary.com/ch/1986/issue10/1029. html.

St. Benedict of Nursia. http://en.wikipedia.org/wiki/Benedict_of_Nursia.

"Syrian Terrorists Behead Catholic Priest." www.nydailynews.com/new/world/ short-syrian-terrorists-behead-catholic-priest-article-1.1387069.

Wild Goose Worship Resources. http://www.iona.org.uk/wgrg_home.php.

Wilson-Hartgrove. *Awakening of Hope: Why We Practice a Common Faith*. Grand Rapids: Zondervan, 2012.

―――. *New Monasticism: What it Has to Say to Today's Church*. Grand Rapids: Brazos, 2008.

―――. *The Wisdom of Stability: Rooting Faith in a Mobile Culture*. Brewster, MA: Paraclete, 2010.